DIG DEEP, STAND TALL

How to Connect with Your Heart
Take the Limits Off of Life
and Finally Reach Your Dreams

Adrian Hayward
Big Culture Books

Dig Deep, Stand Tall: How to Connect with Your Heart, Take the Limits Off of Life, and Finally Reach Your Dreams
by Adrian Hayward

Published by Big Culture Books
https://bigculturebooks.com
admin@bigculturebooks.com

COPYRIGHT NOTICE

DISCLAIMER

Cover by Maša Radanić
Edited and Proofread by Laura Wilkinson
Formatted by Jacqui Corn-Uys

ISBN: 978-1-7398757-0-1
eBook ISBN: 978-1-7398757-1-8

First Edition: December 2021

Download The Audiobook For FREE

CLAIM YOUR FREE GIFT

As a thank you for buying my book, I would like to give you the audiobook version 100% free.

Go to https://digdeepstandtall.com/ddst-free-audiobook-download

To my darling, Clare.

For daring to face it all with me.

Contents

Introduction: When Your Dreams Evade You 1

Part 1: PREP

1 WHEN LIFE MAKES NO SENSE: The Endless Search for Meaning 6

2 WORTH A MILLION WORDS: Understanding Life Through Pictures........... 8

3 GO WIDE, GO TALL: Your Life is a Superstructure 13

4 YOURS AND YOURS ALONE: Own Your Superstructure.......................... 17

Part 2: EVALUATION

5 OPEN THE DOOR TO YOUR HEART: Take That First Look Inside 22

6 SO MANY REASONS TO SHUT THE DOOR: Obstacles You May Encounter When Connecting with Your Heart... 26

7 SURVEY TIME: Perform Your Structural Survey 49

8 ANALYSIS TIME: Complete Your Structural Analysis................................. 57

Part 3: BLUEPRINTS

9 SET YOUR INNER CHILD FREE: Embrace Your Role as Architect in the Process 64

10 THE SKY REALLY IS THE LIMIT: Dare to Dream Like a Child Again 70

11 NO GREATER MOTIVATION: Your 'Why' is Your Reason for Everything 74

12 THE KEY TO REALISING YOUR DREAM LIFE: Your 1/5/10 Plan 78

Part 4: SKILLS

13 YOUR GREATEST SKILL FOR SUCCESS: Never Stop Learning 86

14 WHEN YOUR PARADIGM SHIFTS: Defining Moments When Your Worldview Changes Forever.. 96

15 WHEN LIFE WON'T LET UP: Always Be Prepared 110

16 TAKING CHARGE LIKE A BOSS: The Buck Stops with You 124

Part 5: DIG DOWN DEEP

17 YOUR QUEST FOR STABILITY: Becoming Whole One Day at a Time .142

18 DON'T STOP UNTIL YOU REACH THE BOTTOM: Get to the Heart of the Problem 168

19 MAKE SURE YOU'RE STILL IN IT WHEN YOUR TIME COMES: Win by Staying the Course 186

20 LOOK HOW FAR YOU'VE COME : Reaching Milestone Number One...207

Part 6: GET BUILDING

21 IN THE MEANTIME…: Getting by While You Wait 212

22 THE PERSON YOU'VE BEEN WAITING FOR: Becoming Who You Really Are 220

23 THE PATIENT BUILDER: Tactics to Avoid False Starts...........................224

24 THE MOMENT YOU'VE BEEN WAITING FOR: The Fulfilment of Your Dream 233

Part 7: LASTING CHANGE

25 ONWARDS AND UPWARDS: Now You Own the Process 240

26 FRUITS OF THE PERPETUAL CYCLE: Enjoying the Benefits of Continual Growth 242

27 HOW'S IT LOOKING FROM UP THERE?: Stand Tall, You've Earned it 244

28 SOMETHING TO REMEMBER YOU BY: Leaving a Lasting Legacy 247

Thank you 252

Acknowledgements 253

Author Bio 255

INTRODUCTION

When Your Dreams Evade You

It hurts, doesn't it?

Knowing what you want but not being able to get it.

Your dreams have always been there.

But they're always just out of reach.

And you're left longing for a different life. A life where you wake up excited. A life that you've chosen for yourself. Done *your* way!

Right now, you just feel stuck.

Sometimes it feels like the entire world is against you. You give everything, and all you get is burnt out and depressed.

More and more, you wonder, "What's wrong with me?"

You're not sure how much longer you can keep it up.

So, you're looking for someone to help.

And that's why I'm here.

This is the book I needed as I went through my process to get my life on track. It contains the most important lessons that I learnt along the way.

It's going to show you how to:

1. Connect with your heart
2. Design your life for lasting change
3. Overcome <u>every</u> obstacle you face and…
4. Finally, achieve your wildest dreams

Sounds good, right?

I have spent the last 20+ years learning how to turn dreams into reality while achieving lasting change. I have devoured thousands (literally) of books to build on my understanding. And I've given everything I have to overcome abuse, trauma, addictions, illness, and much more.

I now love my life and want to show you how you can, too.

The understanding in this book will work for anyone, anywhere, including you. And, unlike most advice, the more you've struggled with life so far, the *more* it will help you. I have helped many people get unstuck by sharing this process with them.

This book is for you if you're just starting your journey of self-discovery. It's also for you if you've been at it a while and want to understand why life is still not working the way you'd hoped. It is not a religious book, but it is deeply spiritual because it is all about exploring the deepest parts of your being.

Everything I discuss in this book has been hard-earned. I have lived it all myself and seen it work for many others. The best example of this is my mum. At 69, after many years of being completely stuck in impossibility and unable to find a lasting solution despite her desire to change, she resolved to do whatever it took to get to the core of her problems and is now living a life of fulfilment for the first time.

I can promise you this: this will be the hardest thing you'll ever do, but it will also be the most rewarding. You will feel more alive and enjoy each moment as you rest in the process until it takes you to where you want to be.

As you learn, you will become increasingly confident in your own ability to turn your life around. And if you stick with it, you will never be the same again. Guaranteed!

Sure, you can put it off until New Year's Day, or until you're in your new home. Or until you're 40, or comfortably retired. But you know in your heart that you won't follow through on that.

And you're done with putting it off anyway. Because you want to be the kind of person who achieves. The kind of person who makes the hard decisions now for a brighter future. And the kind of person who gives yourself what you were never given by life and other people.

Choose the dream life you are so desperate for and you won't be disappointed.

Again, the understanding I'm about to share has proven many times to help people turn their lives around, take control, and set them firmly on the path of their choosing. It will help you to face everyone and everything that will come against you, and teach you how to not back down in the face of all adversity.

It will make sense of why other people seem to find life so much easier and don't seem to struggle like you do. It will teach you how to become someone who 'can'.

It's time to take control of your life and finally get the results you deserve.

Let's get started.

PREP

1

WHEN LIFE MAKES NO SENSE
The Endless Search for Meaning

It can be so confusing, can't it?

You're dropped in a world with no manual.

And nobody to explain how it all works.

Just when you think you're finally getting somewhere, life happens and you're back to where you started or nowhere at all.

As day rolls into endless day, you catch yourself thinking more and more, "Is this really all there is?"

But in your heart, you already know the answer.

You *know* there's more.

And something in you says you can have it.

But so far, it's escaped you.

And you can't shake the feeling that you're the only one in the world who can't make life work.

I promise you, you're not.

You're Not Alone

We are all in the same boat, and those who are honest will tell you they don't have a firm handle on life either. They're just learning as they go. Making it up as they go. Everyone is doing the best they can to survive and simply make sense of it all.

Some have been born into circumstances that equip them better for life than others. But a large majority of the world has been born into the same kind of life you have and are longing just as much as you to understand it all.

If you stay with me, I'll prove to you that you've already got everything you need to make your dream life happen.

You've Got What It Takes

I don't know you. But I have an assurance that you've already got what it takes to get wherever your heart desires. Where does this assurance come from?

First, as I've said, I've been through the process myself and had the privilege of seeing others go from nowhere to thriving.

Second, I believe that as a human being, you came equipped with everything you need for life. That you have the same stuff inside you as I do, and no matter how impossible it seems, you can rise above it all and claim what's rightfully yours.

Third, I believe in the power of choice. We'll look at this later. If you choose something, keep choosing it, and don't give up, you will eventually have it.

I believe in you.

And I want to help you believe in yourself.

2

WORTH A MILLION WORDS
Understanding Life Through Pictures

Remember story time when you were little?

What was that book you always asked for?

The one you just had to hear.

Where were you when it was read to you? Tucked up in bed? Or crossed-legged on the mat in first grade?

Fixated on the reader's voice, you pictured every single detail with excitement.

Having heard the story before only made it more exciting. It meant you could anticipate every word just before you heard them.

In fact, the more you'd heard the story, the better. The brighter the images in your mind's eye. And the more real the story seemed.

Because you could see it, you understood it.

And that's still the best way to understand life.

Seeing Life as Pictures

For as long as I can remember, I have seen life in pictures. Not only images in my mind's eye, but word pictures, which allude to something deeper that can help to understand life and the way it works. I'm not sure whether this is an innate thing or something that developed in me over time.

As I've said, one of the best ways to understand life is through pictures. Not the kind that you hang on your wall. But the kind you hold in your heart. That shed light on something hard to grasp when you're looking directly at it.

We love stories when we're younger, not because of the words or concepts themselves, but because of the way they light up our imagination.

The likelihood is, the story you thought of a second ago when I got you to think about when you were younger was about some superhero, cute animal, or robot being. And that's all that drew you to those stories then. But, looking back as an adult, you may see the messages and deep emotions injected by the author that you missed as a child. Even though you weren't conscious of this, you were still responding to it on a deeper level and making sense of the world around you.

Stories like Aesop's fable, *The Tortoise and the Hare,*[1] take it a step further. Their primary purpose is to teach life lessons that are easier to get hold of because of the comparison they make. I'll quickly sum up *The Tortoise and the Hare*, in case you're not familiar:

A hare keeps making fun of a tortoise for his being slow, boasting that he is so much faster.

One day, the tortoise has had enough of it and challenges the hare to a race, telling the hare that he bets he'll be able to beat him. The hare accepts, assuming it will be an easy win since he can move many times faster than the tortoise.

Predictably, as soon as the race starts, the hare tears away from the start line, leaving the tortoise in his dust. He's doing so well that he takes a break. As he rests, he falls asleep and the tortoise overtakes him. By the time the hare wakes, the tortoise is nearing the finish line. The hare runs as fast as he can to catch up, but he's too late and loses the race.

---

[1] Aesop, and George Fyler Townsend. *Aesop's Fables – Complete Collection (Illustrated). 1st ed.* Los Angeles, CA: CreateSpace Independent Publishing Platform, 2016. Kindle.

The *Tortoise and the Hare's* meaning, although slightly ambiguous and widely debated, conveys the life lesson that "slow and steady wins the race".

I call this a life lesson because, although it is about life, it is actually only about one aspect, not the whole.

A step further are parables that give understanding about life as a whole. There are two from the bible that I'm most familiar with because of my Christian upbringing. People commonly refer to these as The Parable of the Sower,[2] and The Wise and Foolish Builders.[3]

There isn't the space to do justice to the depth of understanding in these stories, so I'll let you explore them if you're interested. I'm mentioning them because they are stories that help give an understanding of life from a certain perspective, and because many of the concepts in the two stories appear in this book. Although I have moved away from most of the beliefs of my upbringing, I have not thrown out the parts that have undeniably given me so much and got me to where I am.

I want to make it clear that I am not trying to sell a new way. Throughout history, people have understood everything I'm sharing all around the world. In fact, it was probably understood better then than now. As we've developed in some ways, we've lost touch with other ways that are essential to life. We can recover some of what we've lost.

What I Mean by Picture

There is a type of picture that is produced using a method known as lenticular printing. The effect is that depending on where you're standing in relation to the picture, you see something slightly different. And if you are moving when you look at it, it also appears to move and change.

This is a static image but is also dynamic and has depth.

---

[2] Matt. 13:1–23 NIV
[3] Matt. 7:24–29 NIV

When I say picture, that's what I'm talking about – a picture in your mind that can appear static in one moment and then come to life in the next.

Unlike a parable or fable, this type of picture doesn't have characters or a storyline, but the more you look at the picture and draw comparisons to life, the more understanding you'll get.

If that makes no sense yet, it will.

Three Pictures for Life

There are three pictures I know of for life that are universally understood. Life as a journey, life as a garden, and life as a building. References appear throughout all kinds of literature – religious and non – throughout history. I mentioned the two parables above, which are examples of the latter two.

The journey metaphor is used so often, it has become almost cliché, especially as it is woven into our daily speech: "I've just gotta keep pushing on until I get there." "The finish line is in sight!" And the garden picture is well known and has immense depth, but fewer people have a connection to the earth nowadays in our constantly developing world.

So, that leaves the building picture – which I will call your superstructure from now on because the image is clearer. The superstructure picture is the entire basis for this book and every idea it contains.

This one picture will remind you that you're in a lifelong process that doesn't end until you take your last breath (or maybe beyond. Who knows for sure?). So, by the time you've finished this book, you will have something simple and clear to hold on to in your darkest moments. You'll remember the superstructure you are building and take comfort knowing that the process is always happening. You're either working with it or against it. If you can work in harmony with it, and not give up, you'll finally be able to live a fulfilling life and achieve your wildest dreams.

No one picture can perfectly sum up the whole of life. Once you try to get too specific with comparisons, you draw conclusions that are incorrect. For that reason, there will be many other pictures that I'll draw on – an accumulation of all the concepts that have helped me to get from lost and out of control, to loving life and thriving.

To avoid mixed metaphors, which are always confusing, I will not refer to the journey or garden pictures if I can help it, as they make the same points in different and often conflicting ways.

I will do my best to keep from overusing terminology like superstructure and foundation so it doesn't get repetitive and annoying. And at no point am I wanting to suggest that any of these words have special powers or any meaning beyond being helpful in gaining an understanding of life.

The reason I believe the pictures work so well is that they are not really a metaphor as much as understanding one thing by another because they are both essentially the same. Building a life has the same essential ingredients as building a superstructure. You can see or touch one, and the other is more ethereal, but I believe both are built on the same universal laws. More on this later.

When talking about life, people distinguish between physical, spiritual, heart, soul, etc. I don't want to challenge or debate these. I'll use the best words I have, but please think of these principles in whatever terms work for you.

So, why a superstructure?

3

GO WIDE, GO TALL

Your Life is a Superstructure

But that's not how it feels, is it?

It feels so restrictive and stifling. More of a studio apartment or a two-up, two-down in a rundown part of town, hemmed in on either side with no room to breathe.

Where the council sets the rules and prohibits expansion of any kind. So, your lot is your lot. And that's that.

Where all the resources get diverted to other parts of town and you're left with the scraps.

In your neck of the woods, it's everyone for themselves and you know no one's going to help you even if you're desperate.

It's made worse because you can imagine how things could be different.

So, for now, you just have to make the best of a bad situation.

Right?

You Decide How Big You Go

I really understand how it can look like this. I felt that way for so many years. But your life has the potential to grow to whatever size you want.

It's something that you can build for the rest of your life, as high and as wide as your heart desires. Other people may choose not to. They may like their bungalow, all safe and cosy, and close to the ground. That's great. But, you. You have a desire for more. You have a desire to reach your potential, to learn and grow. To design something exciting. That others can share. That might help people all over the world. To achieve this, there needs to be a special focus on the deeper parts, because that's where the actual issues lie.

Deep But Not Deep Enough

If you do a Google search for answers to a life problem you're facing, you'll find most of the answers relate to above-ground life. How to organise your house, manage your finances, get your relationships in order – above-ground stuff.

When you message the guru on your favourite website whose advice you've been following to tell him it's not working for you, a member of his team comes back and says that you must not be doing it right. You're sure you were. But it must be true. They're the guru, after all. And you're just the person who can't make anything work.

Even where the solutions given are below-ground solutions, they are, more often than not, about stuff just below the surface, like conscious thoughts or mindsets. These *are* the solutions for many people because that's where their issues lie. And there is no value in digging deeper when those things will solve the problem. But if the issues lie deeper and you think you've addressed the core of the problem with a shallow fix, you're in for a shock later when everything falls apart.

In this book, I'll show you that most of your inability to make life work is because of issues going on beneath the surface – below ground – making them structural issues that can affect every part of life. If they remain, your life is in a perpetually precarious state and could come crashing down. Yes, it's possible that it may not, but do you really want to take that risk as you're trying to build something that means so much to you?

The below-ground stuff we are going to be talking about is all the way to the very core of your being. It will not be comfortable, and at times, it will hurt. But, if you want to feel at home in this world and at home with yourself, it is necessary work. What's the point in building a life that looks good on the surface when you don't get to enjoy it?

Whenever you feel like giving up on it, just think – it's a choice between the life you have now, or the life you're dreaming of. If you're honest with yourself, there's no contest.

Above Ground = Good

Despite all the madness and evil in the world, I still believe that life is good. And, I still believe that people are good, which means that I believe you are good and the life you want to create is also good.

I don't believe that one part of life is more important than the other, and I'm never going to suggest that above-ground life is vapid, shallow, or use any other slur. People have given it a bad name because, as we'll see later on, life built on a shallow foundation *is* shallow and won't last. But shallow doesn't mean bad.

Above-ground life is good. Just as a building is not a building without its visible structure, life is not life without the full expression of who we are in action in our daily lives.

Parts of religion and pseudo-spirituality are much to blame for making us feel guilty about wanting things like a spacious home, a fancy car, and luxurious holidays. It had that effect on me.

I became so convinced that the physical world was meaningless, to the point of asceticism, that I gave away and destroyed all my possessions, including trashing all my photos (which still hurts to this day). I really believed the act would help me find true fulfilment and enlightenment. It didn't.

The problem is not that the things we want in life are bad or shameful, it's that on their own, they cannot sustain life and last – the building cannot stand without the foundation. This book is about how to live in integrity, fix the crumbling or cracked foundation, and lay a completely new one, if required. It's about how to extend out. And how to make it strong enough that you can build as high as you ever want to.

I've set the book out following the same order in which a building is constructed. In reality, life isn't that neat. Different areas of your life will be in different stages at the same time and you can have parts not yet started and other parts a mile high.

This book is not a practical (above-ground) guide to life design. There are plenty of those out there already. It won't help you decide what colour to paint your kitchen walls or where to holiday this summer. It's a below-ground guide that teaches you how to draw out your deepest desires and best ideas. This *will* lead in time to you being more equipped to make paint choices and vacation selections, but not directly.

This book is about the stuff most people never talk about – the below-ground/heart stuff. It's about stuff they didn't teach you in school.

How to live your life your way.

4

YOURS AND YOURS ALONE

Own Your Superstructure

You've been told you're not allowed that.

By religion, society, your friends and family.

Everyone with an opinion seems to want to tell you that your purpose for being here is to serve others and give back to the world.

You're surrounded by people that say they know better what you should do with your life.

And it feels like you're being pulled in every direction.

There's no room for your dreams.

There's no room for you.

You Are in Charge

Even though we are all part of the same life, as in the same existence, we are each in charge of our own individual life. The life that you're building is separate and distinct from other people's. You get to decide every aspect and, in superstructure terms, you are the owner, manager, architect, interior designer, security, repair person, and you are fully responsible for every other job necessary to maintain it. You decide it all!

I believe we are all connected to each other and the universe on the deepest level. That we all share in the same life. I don't always like this, but I can't see it any other way.

On the flip side, I believe that we each have our own life – or vital force – completely distinct from other people's meaning, that you and only you are in charge of your life and what happens in it.

If you were raised to believe that you should not think about or want things for yourself, like I was, then it's hard to consider these concepts. But, if you get things straight in your own domain, you will influence the world and people around you for good. In fact, I believe it's the only way to contribute something of value to the world. You can't give what you haven't received. And, if nobody gave it to you in the first place, you're going to have to give it to yourself first.

When I came to the realisation over 20 years ago that I needed to transform every aspect of my life in order to stand any chance of achieving my dreams, I had no idea what I was getting into. If I had known how hard the process would be or how long it would take, I would probably have not even got started. But, thankfully, I just held on a little longer, and then a little longer again, until I reached where I am now. Life is a marathon, not a sprint.

One of the hardest things about my process in the early days was learning that I needed to take responsibility and make it happen, even though I hadn't chosen a lot of what I was stuck with. If this is an issue you struggle with, I really get it. And I want you to know that you really can move past it.

My greatest desire is to show you how to live an autonomous life, building higher and wider than you could ever imagine possible, and achieve everything your heart desires. I'm inviting you on an adventure to explore the depths of your being until you start to feel whole and comfortable with who you are. So that you wake up in the morning feeling at peace with yourself, and when you look in the mirror, you actually like the person staring back at you. Like every adventure, it has its risks and no end of challenges. But it also leads to life. Your life. Your superstructure.

Right, that's enough prep.

Let's get going.

EVALUATION

5

OPEN THE DOOR TO YOUR HEART
Take That First Look Inside

How does it feel?

When you stop for a second or a minute. No phone to distract you. No TV on. Just you and your thoughts and feelings.

You open the door to your inner world and step in. Everything comes into focus. Does it feel easy? Or do you squirm a little because it's so uncomfortable, or worse, intolerable?

Unless you were brought up in a family and culture that showed you the value of solitude and silence and how to feel at ease with yourself, looking inside may be one of the hardest things you'll ever do. And I mean *the* hardest.

Why? Because there are good reasons you've learned to avoid it. Because when you look for even a second, you face the clutter that's built up, and the damage done to you over the course of your life. The easiest thing to do is to close the door and ignore it.

But on some level, you know it's not going away on its own. And that's why you're still with me.

Because you want to face this stuff once and for all. Because you want the good life that's calling your name.

You want that change.

But where do you start?

Start Where You Are

Starting where you are is a simple concept to grasp because, in reality, it's all you can do and there are no other options. But we have ways of twisting and contorting things to make them feel easier. So, we try to be anywhere but where we really are. Nothing actually changes, but we convince ourselves of whatever it is we would rather believe about ourselves, and that makes us feel better.

For years, I tried to be a few steps ahead of where I was. I didn't know how to accept the mess my life was in and didn't want to be seen as a screw-up, so I continually pushed on, ignoring the many struggles that were holding me back. In the end, I burnt myself out and am still recovering. In reality, I always was where I was and no contortion of the facts was ever going to change that.

You are where you are, whether you recognise or like it. Or not. But you will feel more at ease if you allow yourself to come to terms with it. This is one of the primary principles of change.

Most advice out there on how to change starts with the destination in mind. But that's the easy and fun part. You probably have ideas that have been with you for years about where you want to end up. Just as important (maybe more so) is to recognise and build a picture of where you are now. This is going to give you a solid base to work from and keep you from getting trapped in dreams about the future without ever following through.

All life flows from deep inside you, and if there's a blockage or a crack deep inside, it has the potential to stop that inner life from becoming life on the outside.

Your life is not completely of your own making. Your parents gave you it. And, with it, you inherited many attributes – some desirable, some not – that make up part of who you are today. Throughout your life up to this point, people have contributed aspects to your life which may have helped to make you strong, or may have been the reason you can't get anything to remain standing in your life. Some people have smashed their way in and dumped their trash everywhere. Others have tried to influence or control your decisions because of their idea of what's right and what's best for you.

These experiences conditioned you to favour certain choices and hold certain viewpoints that then dictate the state of your life. If you have been making choices in line with your conditioning without realising it, this is a very hard thing to face up to, but it is not something that you can avoid if you want to change.

So, that's what we're going to do. Face up to everything inside. Starting with where you are now.

In a few pages, we're going to perform an exercise we're calling 'Your Structural Survey'. I know that may not sound exciting. And, the survey itself isn't. But what it will tell you about yourself and your life is.

The primary aim of *Your Structural Survey* is to give you a clear picture of where you are now.

What State Are You in <u>Right Now</u>?

In property development, the order is: survey, then plan. You don't make the plans and then do the survey because the survey reveals things you'll need for your plan. Because they are deep and hidden. So, that's where we're going to start this process. Using your survey to get a clear picture of where you are now.

Here's a definition of structural survey:

"A structural survey (often referred to as a building survey) is a comprehensive inspection of a property to provide a detailed evaluation of its condition. Structural surveys outline the condition of each element of the house or commercial property

and highlight areas that may need further investigation or any areas that are a cause for concern."[4]

We're calling the exercise we're about to do a structural survey because that's exactly what it is on a heart level – taking the time to inspect the parts of your life that matter most so you can clearly see the areas that need more focus and attention, and the areas that need immediate action.

Without judgement.

No Judgement Here

This survey is designed to help and not hurt you. This means no judgement. We're simply going to notice whatever draws our attention and make no value statements like, 'I'm so rubbish,' or, 'I hate the way I'm…' Just notice whatever you notice. The state of your life is what it is, and that's OK, for now. That doesn't mean we're going to leave it that way. But, for now, it is OK.

And there will be no judgement from me. It's impossible for me to judge you because of where I've come from. I can't imagine how I could have been more messed up and unable to produce the results I wanted. So, I am your friend and your ally in this. Nothing else.

I would like you to make a commitment that you will not judge yourself for where you find yourself to be. As we talked about a minute ago, a lot of the reason you are where you are is not actually your doing. We'll look at that more later. If you've learnt to judge yourself and it's an ingrained habit, I know one commitment will not stop you from doing it. But if you commit to it, you've stated your intention to yourself and taken one step. This is the basis for all change. This is the basis for this book.

OK, I think we're ready. Hard hats on. We're going inside.

---

[4] Admin. "What Is a Structural Survey?" Green Structural Engineering, gseltd.co.uk. January 20, 2017. www.gseltd.co.uk/what-is-a-structural-survey.

6

SO MANY REASONS TO SHUT THE DOOR

Obstacles You May Encounter When Connecting with Your Heart

You open the door to your heart and step inside.

As you lift your head, something comes into focus.

And then, ping, your phone screams at you – you've got a message.

You glance down and see that it's just a work chat group.

So, you close your eyes to focus harder and try to notice what it was you were glimpsing before.

And then, you hear a voice in your head, saying, "I wonder what's on TV tonight."

You shake yourself to get back to the moment and then there's a knock at the door and it's a family member with a question.

They look at you weirdly and ask what you're doing. You fob them off, and once they've left, get back to it.

This time, you clearly see what had caught your attention. It's pain. Just pain. You shut your inner door, pick up your phone, check your email and social media while turning the TV to any channel.

Anything to avoid the pain.

So Many Obstacles

We all go through this. I lived like this for many years, even when I was already digging deep. Like anything, it takes practice and courage, and we need to learn that looking inside our heart is safe and that it won't hurt us.

Next, we're going to take the time to look at the things that can impede *Your Structural Survey* and your ability to connect with your heart. The reason it's so important is that unless we learn to identify the obstacles, we can keep telling ourselves that we don't have the time or the space to look inside and take stock. When, in reality, we welcome most of the obstacles because they give us a reason not to look inside.

Let's look at what some of these obstacles are.

External Obstacles

Distractions

As in the example above, it's things like the phone, the TV, the knock at the door. And much more. I know you're aware of them already but you may not be fully aware of how much they are within your control, even when it's other people doing the distracting.

An example from my life is that until recently, the doorbell ringing at my flat triggered me massively into flashback. The solution to this was that unless my fiancée, Clare, or I were expecting a parcel or visitor, we turned it off. There is no law that says your doorbell has to be on. Same with the mobile phone. When Clare and I go on holiday, we switch off our mobiles when we leave our place, and turn on a cheap emergency phone that just does calls and texts. Only our parents have the number and know that someone needs to be dying, and not expected to survive the end of the holiday, for us to be disturbed (semi-seriously). Point is, there is nothing more important for us than that one week a year when we can switch off and just *be*, so we proactively prevent the distraction.

Do what you need to do to stop these external distractions before they happen.

Resistance from Others

There's an entire section devoted to this later on (*Going Against the Tribe*), so I'll keep it brief here. Other people, even family and friends, can be the greatest force against our change. They may not mean to be, and it might horrify them to hear it, but it's true. The most common reason is that the thing you are doing challenges them and makes them feel uncomfortable. As long as you're being considerate, this is not your problem.

In the example above, a family member knocks on the door, letting themselves in and gives you a funny look because you are just sitting there. That one funny look is enough to derail your process when you're just getting started. You need to protect your life process with everything in you, especially when you're just starting out because it's so fragile and new.

We put covers around a sapling and wrap a baby in our arms to protect them from harm.

That's how you need to be with this process.

For that reason, at first, I recommend only sharing about this process with those you know are in tune with you and supportive of you trying new things. It's just too easy to be brought back to square one or even zero because of one flippant comment.

For now, keep it safe and keep it to yourself.

Where You're From

If you look around and all you see is people stuck in the same old same old, it can have such a powerful effect on you that it keeps you from ever breaking free. In the UK, it may be the council estate you're from, or being from a 'benefits family' in receipt of social security. Maybe it's your family religion or ethnicity. Or, maybe your country doesn't have the resources available, and when you look around, you can't see any hope. Even though I was raised in relative poverty, I'm from the UK, so I haven't experienced things to the degree you may have. There are many accounts of people that have come from nothing to turn their lives around. It may take ingenuity, invention, innovation and massive amounts of courage. But, one thing for sure is that it is never impossible.

For me, one of the strongest images that was burnt into my little mind as a kid was my dad going to work for the council in his fluorescent jacket, depressed and unmotivated. The other one was my mum at the sink, tired and in pain, seeing every aspect of life as an impossible mountain to climb. The combination of these two memories has left me with a confusing sense that it would be a betrayal of my roots and upbringing to make something of myself. It sounds crazy to say it, but that is how it feels.

'Starting from nothing' is a common phrase, which means nobody gave us what we needed to get going in life. But, the concept is actually never accurate. If our parents and environments had given us nothing, we'd be dead already or incapable of functioning. They gave us a lot, even though that can be hard to admit. The other side of this is that with some things they gave us, it would be better if they hadn't at all. So, it's not so much starting with nothing but starting with a lot that is working against us and standing in our way, hampering progress.

Where you're from never dictates where you can go and, most of all, who you are and who you can become. But where you start definitely makes some difference to how your life will play out.

Don't ignore it. But don't let it decide your future either.

Issues with What I'm Saying

You're only just getting to know me. And only through my words. You're right to be on guard and uncertain whether to trust the things I'm saying. You *should* protect yourself in that way. There will be times where what I say grates against you or you're absolutely certain that I'm wrong. That's OK! I *am* often wrong. I'm not trying to convince you that what I believe is right. I'm simply trying to share ideas that have helped me and hope will help you too. They're not my ideas. They've been around forever. But, I may not convey them in the best way and I may have understood them wrongly or incompletely.

So, if it doesn't resonate, we don't need to fall out over it. Just ask yourself, 'Is this because I don't agree with what he's saying, or is it because I don't like what he's saying as it challenges me?' Either answer is fine. The first means there is something I could learn from you and I'll happily take it. The second means you may need to move from your position to find a better way.

Because that's what leads to more life.

Internal Obstacles

Distractions

You will need to deal with these differently to external distractions because you can't shut them out in the same way.

One of the biggest internal distractions is wondering or interrupting thoughts. The best technique I know of for this is to write them down on a piece of paper, intending to deal with them later. Capturing these thoughts on paper can help you relax and forget about them because you know you can come back to what you've written later if need be. And the good thing is, it still frees your mind even if you don't.

The internal distraction I struggle with the most is brain fog because of trauma and chronic fatigue. Sometimes my mind simply won't function, like someone has poured treacle into the gears and everything is set on go slow. The only solution I know for this is to rest until I am in a better place.

Be kind to yourself and try to understand what's behind these internal distractions.

Difficult Emotions

If you've not been in touch with your feelings much, you may not feel comfortable with them. That's OK! As we've already discussed, there's no judgement in this process. Just allow all feelings to be what they are and try to see what you can notice about them.

Despite appearances, there is no such thing as a bad emotion. Society has conditioned us to seek after certain kinds of emotions and avoid others. This is true no matter what culture you are from.

Every emotion has its place and purpose. Like a warning light in a car, so-called bad emotions can actually tell us when something is wrong.

Anxiety says we are hungry or need the toilet. Fear says to avoid something that may harm us. Anger tells us someone has violated our boundaries. Loneliness tells us we need other people. Dissatisfaction says it's time for a change. We may put a bit of tape over the warning light and ignore it for a while, but eventually, the thing it's pointing to is going to cause problems anyway.

In his book, *The Tao of Fully Feeling*, Psychotherapist and C-PTSD survivor Pete Walker says:

"Many people experience the emotions of grief as a series of waves interspersed with troughs of calm. These waves can come as unpredictably as they do in the ocean. For survivors of long-term abuse, there may be a great many waves. Sometimes there are long periods of tranquility between them, and sometimes it feels as if there is nothing but wave after wave. And sometimes the waves are small and relatively easy to ride, and sometimes they are big "dumpers" that keep us submerged in grief much longer than we would like."[5]

We can't control the waves. We can't prolong the 'good' ones and avoid the ones we'd rather not face, but we can learn to ride them and let them be what they are.

Wholeness doesn't mean becoming perfect, it means embracing the whole of ourselves – warts and all. There is no way to be truly whole or fully engage with life without all our emotions. They truly are the spice of life.

Many of us struggle to cry or express anger. This gives us little outlet for the things we are feeling. Crying and angering are two of the greatest tools we have to deal with unresolved trauma. The combination of learning to cry and learning to anger things out has brought about the most transformation in my life. As I allow myself to feel and express what

---

[5] Walker, Pete. *The Tao of Fully Feeling: Harvesting Forgiveness out of Blame. 2nd ed.* Lafayette, CA, Azure Coyote Book. 2015. Kindle.

I felt and feel about the things that happened throughout my life, I can let them go and then, at some point, the emotions I've been longing for like peace, joy, contentment wash over me.

As a 40-year-old man, I find it so hard that facing up to some childhood issues can cause me to cry like a baby. It's humbling. But, also completely worth it to be rid of emotions that have tormented me my whole life.

What I've never gotten used to is that, after times where I have felt and remembered all the worst stuff that happened to me, would follow moments of feeling amazing. As I've been writing this section, I remembered a horrific new memory and faced it. The result is I feel a brightness I don't remember feeling for a moment in my life before.

Emotions are your friend. All of them. Embrace them.

Too Many Voices

For many years, I experienced auditory hallucinations which occurred as different voices inside or outside myself that continually fought for my attention. Each voice had a unique personality – some were kind, and some were frightening. I was so bombarded by my experience of this that I found it impossible to function and did everything I could to distract myself. In time, I came to the place where I could face them and gradually saw that those voices were all unprocessed events and emotions bouncing around inside me with nowhere to go. I wasn't crazy after all.

In the last year, I have been doing a new form of psychotherapy called IFS, which stands for Internal Family Systems.[6] The 'family' part of the name is the family of parts or sub-personalities inside each of us, not our nuclear family. This family comprises the Self, which is incorruptible and

[6]Schwartz, Richard, and Martha Sweezy. *Internal Family Systems Therapy, Second Edition*. New York, NY: The Guilford Press. 2020. Kindle.

unbreakable, and Parts – Exiles, Managers, and Firefighters which have come about because of trauma and the need for protection.

Exile parts come to be because of trauma, neglect and shame. Manager parts proactively protect the entire system by being prepared and keeping it stable. And the Firefighter parts reactively jump in to protect the entire system from the pain the Exiles carry.

When I first encountered IFS, it was a paradigm shift moment. I had heard the concept of having an inner child many times, but that never helped me understand what was going on inside me because it is a singular concept. IFS made sense of the complexity that I experienced within myself. All those parts came to be because of the things I suffered. But more importantly, they were not evil and destructive as I had seen them for many years. Every part was trying to help and protect me. And – this is one of the most important messages of IFS – there are no bad parts. If only I'd known that in my 20s and 30s. I could have been kinder and more understanding towards myself.

For many years, I wondered: "Which me is me?" The answer to that was and is: all of them.

Your experience may not be the same as mine, but it may be helpful to adopt the IFS' view of having many parts to make sense of your internal world. I love it because it matches the complexity within us, and gives a depth of understanding that terms like 'ego' and 'inner child' don't offer.

I highly recommend IFS if you want to get to know your many parts.

To learn more about it, check out: https://ifs-institute.com.

Have Nots

It's so easy to focus on what you don't have rather than what you do. This kind of view can set you up for a fall because it fills you with impossibility about even getting started.

One enormous obstacle to getting started is the feeling that you don't have any idea how to change. This is a valid concern, but not one that needs to be a permanent obstacle. In her book of the same name, Marie Forleo says that "Everything is figureoutable."[7] This is a powerful truth because it means you are ready now. You don't need to know anything going into this process. You can find it all out along the way.

Focus on your haves and remember: Everything is figureoutable.

Doubts

Do you feel completely unsure of yourself and the world around you?

Don't worry, that's where a lot of us find ourselves all the time. Even though doubts are hard to deal with and feel like they might stop you in your tracks, they are just temporary and things can swing to the opposite extreme in the same hour. The key with doubts is to take them seriously and try to understand where they are coming from. They are not your enemy. They are raising questions about whether something makes sense, whether it's possible, whether you have what it takes. All completely valid questions.

Don't be afraid of doubts. They can point the way forward.

Impossibility

This is the word that sums up where I came from so I know what it looks, feels, and smells like. To have the cards stacked against you, where every single thing you do to change collapses before your eyes. But impossibility is always an illusion because this world has infinite possibilities. Even though it feels like it sometimes, we have never tried everything and there is always more we can learn.

One of the best things I ever learnt about this was from a talk by a man named Andre Rabe. In his gentle South African accent, he said, "Certainty

---

[7] Forleo, Marie. *Everything Is Figureoutable*. New York, NY: Penguin. 2019. Kindle.

is the enemy of possibility." (Did you do the accent?) I have said that to myself so many times since, when it looked like I had nowhere to go.

Certainty equals taking the position that there is only one possibility and, with that one viewpoint, we go from infinite to one. Certainty limits our lives and guarantees a single outcome. If that outcome is not one we want, then life can get pretty miserable, fast.

Those memories of my dad and mum I mentioned earlier in relation to work were full of impossibility and, to this day, affect me. Even though for years I've worked hard on trying to nail the housework, for example, every time I come to do the dinner and the washing up, I still feel this impossibility bearing down on me like a tonne of bricks. Then, suddenly, I've done the job, and I am shocked that I got it done so quickly. My siblings and I laugh because my mum frequently uses the phrase: "It's so easy." This is her realisation every time she achieves something that, for decades, seemed like the hardest thing in the world. Every time, it's still a shock to her.

Addiction is one of the biggest impossibilities that I have faced. It is all-pervasive and doesn't let up. But the impossibility of it is an illusion. I know you may be thinking about your own addiction right now and wondering, "What does he know?" But I do know what that impossibility looks like more than most. If addiction feels like a never-ending spiral, you're probably going to need some help. There is a load out there when you're ready.

In no way does addiction have to be an obstacle to this process. In fact, it's a part of the process, and staying with it can give you what you need to see the back of it. Forever.

Impossibility is a self-imposed prison. We may not have put ourselves there, but we keep ourselves there by not allowing the infinite possibilities to disrupt where we are now.

Open yourself up to the infinite possibilities available to you and you will see there's no end to what you can achieve.

Resistance

Everyone who goes through this process feels resistance. I don't believe that anyone naturally likes this kind of change. And nobody faces their deepest, darkest parts over watching the football, shopping with friends or partying. We will go into more detail about this later, but that resistance, which can feel like the most powerful force in the world, is actually your friend. Once you understand this, it will be easier to ride it out.

Be patient and you will eventually get past even the toughest resistance.

Blindness

In the epic movie, *The Lord Of The Rings: The Two Towers*,[8] there is a scene where Gandalf – a good wizard – frees King Théoden from a spell that he had been placed under for many years by the evil Saruman. While under the spell, he was also under the control of Saruman.

When Gandalf says the words, "I release you from this spell," what follows is like an exorcism of sorts, which culminates in King Théoden shedding the effects that the spell had on him in the space of seconds, making him appear decades younger. Once the spell has worn off, he looks at his niece who is now by his side and says, "I know your face."

While under the spell, he could not see what was right in front of him.

And once the spell was broken, it was like the old hymn says, "was blind but now I see."[9]

---

[8] The Lord Of The Rings: The Two Towers. Directed by Peter Jackson, Extended Edition. NYC: New Line Cinema, 2002.
[9] Newton, John. Amazing Grace. 1779.

When we are blind to something, we are actually incapable of seeing. It appears to be ignorance or stupidity and other people can't understand why we can't get hold of something so simple. But it is rarely our choice or fault. In some cases, we were born that way or became that way very early on. Sometimes someone has blinded us because it suits them. And sometimes we blind ourselves because seeing is too painful or dangerous.

This process will gradually restore your sight, revealing glimpses of new and different ways. The more you see, the more you'll see. And so on. Until, one day, you realise you can't now see in the way you used to and you are free.

Allow yourself time to recover your sight. It's often not your fault that you can't see something, and it is usually a result of trauma.

Avoidance

Do you bury your head in the sand rather than face things head-on? That's completely natural. We all wish we lived in a world where there was nothing we had to face up to. But avoidance can be the very reason we are where we are. Once we realise this, it's easier to look at things that we have shied away from.

Avoidance is what I described earlier – walking through the door of your heart, not liking what you've seen, and simply walking out and closing the door on it again. No matter how long you stay away, though, the mess is still going to be there when you walk back in. In fact, it may even be worse.

Life requires your full attention to work. As you learn mindfulness through this process, you can learn to face up to even the hardest things and keep facing them until they resolve.

Limiting Beliefs

"I can't do that," "I'm not confident enough," "I don't have her talents," "I'm not very bright."

These are all limiting beliefs. As are a lot of the other obstacles we've just covered.

"Whether you believe you can do a thing or not, you are right."[10]

What we believe about ourselves either sets us up for success or for failure before we've even started. If you believe you absolutely cannot do something, you won't even attempt it, or if you do, you will fulfil the prophecy by subconsciously sabotaging the thing and so prove your belief. If you believe you can, even with no basis for it, the chances are you will find a way to do that thing.

There is a lot of woo-woo out there. It is not enough to simply 'believe' something. As you'll see going through the rest of this book, belief is just one element that leads to success. But one thing's for sure, if you absolutely believe you cannot do something, you almost certainly won't.

Take the limits off of your thinking and you will take the limits off of your life.

Perfectionism

Do you know this one? I certainly do. You've just got to keep going a little more so that you can finish that last bit and then it will be… perfect. But you finish that bit and you realise there's that other part over there that needs some improvement. It eats away inside you and makes you feel sick. But you're sure you're nearly there. Just a bit more.

---

[10]O'Toole, Garson. "Whether You Believe You Can Do a Thing or Not, You Are Right." Quote Investigator, www.quoteinvestigator.com, February 3, 2015, quoteinvestigator.com/2015/02/03/you-can.

Perfectionism is a delusion that aims for faultless results and isn't willing to settle for anything less. The actual result is almost always mediocre. Excellence, however, is aiming for the best *you* (not it) can be, and being satisfied when *it* turns out to be good.

Perfectionism guarantees the kind of crushing failure where you fall short of the expected mark and there's nothing you can do about it.

Self-development still guarantees failure but a different kind. It leaves room for the failures you can learn from and even allows you to build failure in for greater success.

Another form of perfectionism that I have fallen into is, "If I can't do it perfectly, then I won't do it at all." This leaves us nothing to point to, which feels like a massive failure. Since perfection is impossible, this is a kind of stalemate that you can only break by accepting a good outcome as good enough.

Good enough is my favourite antidote to perfectionism. Or, "*Done* is better than perfect." That's my mantra for this book. Many have said it. But, most recently, I heard it from Chandler Bolt – CEO of Self-Publishing School – about getting your book written and out there. As I type the first draft, I am refusing to critique or edit as I go so that, in a few short weeks, I'll have reached a major milestone that will be good enough. If I had let the editor in my head loose for even a minute, I'd still be in chapter one instead of six.

Good enough does not mean mediocre, it means great! It's not the ultimate aim, but is the best you can give while you wait for yourself to become even better. It keeps you learning and creating and putting stuff out into the world.

Aim for good enough as you continually learn how to better yourself.

Comparison

"Look at her, I wish I had her body!"

"He doesn't even try, and he gets a promotion. And, I've been here three years longer than him."

"All my friends are married with babies already. And they're all younger than me."

There are two main types of comparison – helpful and unhelpful. All the comparisons above are unhelpful because, although they seem to compare like with like, there are many hidden differences that separate those being compared.

The last example is my own. All of my closest friends are married and all but a couple have children already. At points, I wondered, 'What's wrong with me that I'm so behind them?' As I gained clarity, I realised there is a lot that separates us – they had relatively secure upbringings, nobody severely abused or neglected them, they developed enough self-esteem to believe that someone would want to be with them, and they didn't doubt they could have what they wanted.

Unhelpful comparison is: Comparing yourself with people who have what you want, comparing yourself with people who haven't faced what you've faced, comparing to people who had a different start to you, comparing your struggles with other people's, either to say that what they went through was worse or better.

In this book, I am trying to avoid triggering unhelpful comparison with my examples. This happens when other people learn something through years of hard learning and then share it in three minutes, saying, "Do what I did…" Or, "Don't do what I did…" Unfortunately, it's not that simple. Sometimes we just have to learn for ourselves and sometimes we just gotta learn the hard way.

Helpful comparison is comparison with who you once were when done in a non-judgemental way. You can say, "I was in a total mess five years ago and now I have a job and can handle my finances for the first time." This shows progress, which is helpful.

A common tool that helps measure this kind of progress has names like 'Success Wheel', 'Wheel of Life' and 'Life Balance Wheel'. It looks a bit like a pie chart divided into equal triangular sections, like pizza slices. Each section represents an area of your life like personal growth, romantic relationship, business and career, and fun and recreation. Periodically, you score each area out of 10 to reflect your current state. The more balanced your life is, the more it looks like a wheel. But if you have some areas where you score a 1 or 2 and some that you score a 9 or 10, it looks nothing like a wheel, which represents the imbalance in your life.

By completing the wheel exercise every few months or once a year, you can measure progress – rather than trusting your own perception on the fly, which is really hard to do.

For a great explanation of how to create your own Wheel of Life, check out: https://scottjeffrey.com/wheel-of-life.

A grey area for me is comparing with other people in similar circumstances. You could call this statistical comparison. This is how it goes: "Since nine of my friends have died because of their addictions, and I'm still here, I'm doing pretty well." Or, "Most of the people I know with mental health issues haven't got as far as I have." These are personal examples. Statistically, it would be no surprise if I'd died years ago. It would be even less surprising if I was still struggling the same way I was years ago. But I'm not sure if that's a helpful comparison or not.

Despite my uncertainty, sometimes looking at where I could have ended up helps bring some perspective. Although I'm not where most of my close friends are, who received more stable upbringings, I'm doing pretty well coming from where I've come from.

Only compare yourself to yourself and only in ways that are constructive.

Trauma

Someone or something hurt you. It wasn't your fault. You didn't choose it. Or maybe you're unsure about that last point. You think you did make some choices that led to you getting hurt. That feels really confusing and may make you wonder whether it *is* all your fault. Either way, you're hurt. And that hurt won't go away on its own.

Trauma is a natural emotional response to something bad that's happened to you. It could have come from abuse, neglect, being bullied, the death of a loved one, a car crash or many other events. The event does not dictate how extreme the trauma will be. It's all relative. Some people develop an ability to handle extreme situations relatively unscathed, whereas others have no defences against something that even they consider to be mild in the grand scheme of things, and when compared to others. There's no value in comparing your trauma with someone else's. If you were traumatised, you were traumatised. You need healing. You need help.

I've left this obstacle until last because it is the most important and the least understood. This is true despite all the progress in recent decades to understand trauma better.

For a war veteran injured in battle, something unrelated like picking up their child or diving into a pool can aggravate their wound. In the same way, everyday occurrences can trigger your inner wounds. This can make you feel unhinged when it happens because your reactions and the way you feel seem so disconnected from what's going on in the moment. But there really isn't anything wrong with you. That's just how trauma works.

I went to the dentist yesterday, and as I was lying in the chair having my tooth drilled, it triggered memories of horrific abuse from when I was younger. I also flashed back to extremely traumatic dentist appointments, where the injection didn't work and I could feel the drill bouncing off my nerve. On the way back home, I had a panic attack on the train, which was the first I'd experienced in years. Thankfully, I managed to ground myself in the moment and came out of it without too much fallout.

Just a year ago, I had no capacity to distinguish between those flashbacks and reality. It shows how much can change in a relatively short space of time.

When the trauma takes place during our formative years, it sets up a paradigm and we are hard-wired to see life according to that paradigm. A couple of years ago, I reached a place of being strong enough to remember an incident that shaped my entire life when I was four. My dad pinned my mum against the living room door and attacked her, punching and kicking her as hard as he could. She thought he was going to kill her because he was so angry. I froze with fear and had no way to escape because they were blocking the door.

After the attack, which was brought on by my mum defending me from my dad, she was trying to get me away from him and they were both pulling me backwards and forwards. I knew they were arguing about me, and my four-year-old interpretation was that this meant I had to choose between them – choose which one I loved the most.

From that point on, the freeze response became my dominant response and every decision I faced felt like a life or death decision. Also, I would experience unbearable feelings of being trapped but couldn't verbalise them.

Once I was ready to face this memory, those confusing feelings suddenly made perfect sense.

It has taken years to make connections like this and be able to understand what is going on in my mind and body. For so long, I was just stuck in endless cycles of being triggered, with feelings that were completely unbearable, and finding substances to block the memories and the pain. But I didn't know that's what was happening then. I had no clue what was going on.

My dentist example is fairly easy to understand because most people find the dentist slightly traumatising. But when you're sitting in a cafe, having coffee and cake with your best friend, and out of nowhere you feel as though you're getting beaten, or worse, and believe your friend or someone else is out to get you, it's very confusing. If you don't see the trigger or make the connection, then you can't make sense of what's going on and it feels completely real, as though it's actually happening in that moment. The trigger may have been the look on someone's face or a joke or even a smell. And a part of your brain activates to protect you from ever having to suffer what you did before. It's working *for* you, but it rarely feels like it because it can cause such disruptive and destructive outcomes and behaviours.

Flashbacks are memories that don't have a date and time stamp. Our brain never filed them in our long-term memory, so every time they come up, it's as though what we're remembering is happening right now, and we relive the experience again and again.

No one could help me process any of the abuse I suffered when I was younger. The church we attended didn't think it was right to get help from outside, but didn't offer an alternative. So, the trauma went around and around in me, unprocessed for 30 years.

If you have experienced trauma that remains unresolved, get help. This is not something to be taken lightly and deserves your attention. Get all the help you can. Where? Wherever you can. If you have access to therapy and can afford it, then start there. But, if you don't, like I didn't for a long time, learn as much as you can from books and the internet. Find people you trust enough to share something with, however small.

I went most of my life without being able to recall a particular abuse from when I was younger. My brain had blocked the memories out to protect me because they were so horrific and I didn't have the capacity or tools to deal with them. Afterwards, I didn't feel I had a safe enough adult that I could trust to tell about what had happened to me. This left me with an unbearable burden to carry.

I wasn't able to factor the abuse into why my life was such a mess and why I couldn't get anywhere because I had no memory of it happening. I didn't understand why I drank and took drugs like I did. Why most days, for many years, I had to fight to stay alive and not take my own life. Wanting to get beneath the behaviour and get to the root, my brother asked me why I did these things, but I could never find an answer for why. I had locked them up tight.

For me, understanding trauma and its role in my life has been the greatest key to unlocking my potential. I am only writing these words because enough healing has taken place and I am strong enough to share my experience. Just a few months ago, I couldn't go out on my own. I stayed in with the curtains closed because any light hurt my eyes. Every little sound triggered a flashback. And all night long I would face flashback after flashback, feeling like one disaster after another was about to happen at any moment. I couldn't even see my friends because I just didn't have it in me.

Today, I am tired from not sleeping much but I'm getting on with the day. I have pain in my body but it's less than it ever was. I can gaze out the window at the autumn light and appreciate its beauty. The sounds of people in the surrounding flats don't bother me as much and don't prevent me from writing. Although these things may not sound like much to some, I know you understand because those are the kinds of changes you're looking for in the areas that matter most to you. I want you to have those changes, too.

A lesser known type of flashback is the emotional flashback.[11] I have suffered with these for many years as well. They are a common symptom of Complex-PTSD. The fundamental difference with these types of flashback is that they rarely have a visual element. The experience I described above about being out for a coffee with a friend is the kind of thing I'm talking about. Suddenly, something triggers me and the emotions of the past trauma are superimposed over (or under) the current situation. Before I understood this, I would genuinely believe that my friend was manipulating me or trying to kill me because the feeling was so strong. Now I have reached a place where I can mostly tell that I am in flashback and need to get out of it.

Something that often points to unresolved trauma is pain in your body. It can mean there's something you've learnt over time to ignore and it's rattling around inside you with nowhere to go. Like a warning light, it is trying to get your attention to say there is something more serious you need to deal with. Sometimes, the more you ignore it, the worse it becomes until you can't ignore it anymore. I still default to thinking that pain or discomfort in my body results from a lack of exercise or something I've eaten. But then I'll face up to something and let it go, usually by crying, and the physical symptoms vanish.

What might your symptoms be pointing to?

If something like this comes up during *Your Structural Survey*, just recognise it and write it down. Just doing this will make a difference.

Do not tackle it yet unless you already know what you're doing.

OK, that's the obstacles covered.

In the next chapter, I'll introduce *Your Structural Survey* and then we'll get going. See you over there.

---

[11] Walker, Pete. *Complex PTSD: From Surviving to Thriving: A Guide and Map for Recovering from Childhood Trauma. 1st ed.* Lafayette, CA: Azure Coyote Publishing. 2013. Kindle

7

SURVEY TIME

Perform Your Structural Survey

You're reading a good book.

And the author gives you an exercise to do.

You go to read on, but in the next line, they say, "Do not skip this vital step... or else!"

What do you do?

If you're like me, you skip it anyway.

But as you move on, there's this nagging thought at the back of your mind that, by skipping that step, you've probably ruined your chances of success.

After all, she said it was a vital step.

You Do It Your Way

I won't pressure you.

If I suggest anything in this book, it's a suggestion. There will be times I say things are really important, but I'm talking more about principles that we all need to grapple with. You decide what's right for you.

Your Structural Survey contains questions and prompts. You'll only get the full benefit of the exercises by participating in them. But if you have a way that works better for you, go for it. And, if you just want to read it through, that's fine.

You do your thing.

Right, before you get your survey out, I just want to cover a few things.

Your Structural Survey and the subsequent two chapters are deliberately short and as simple as they can be. But don't let this fool you. They are extremely powerful. The main reason I've kept them simple is so that you can do them quickly since they will give you the most benefit when used regularly.

I have used these tools or variations of them throughout the years and they have helped to turn my life around. When Clare and I go through the exercises together, we get our little whiteboard out, do each exercise, take a picture, then wipe the board and move on to the next part of the exercise. It's a fun way to do it.

If you want to supplement these exercises, there are plenty of other resources out there that can help you with looking inside and getting to know yourself. One of the main types is personality tests, which help you gain an understanding of your general combination of personal attributes. Myers-Briggs is the most well-known but you can also find free versions like https://www.16personalities.com and https://personalitypath.com to get you started. You'll definitely be able to find something that resonates with you.

If you already have other practices, that's great. Otherwise, concepts you can search for online are journaling, mind-mapping, freewriting, meditation, and mindfulness.

When doing the exercises in this book, you can write, type, draw, speak into a voice recorder, or just do them in your head.[12]

The workbook on the next page is *Your Structural Survey*. Trust the process and just allow whatever comes up.

---

[12] For help understanding your learning preference, check out https://vark-learn.com.

**If you'd like a fillable/printable PDF workbook containing the three exercises
from this book, you can download it here:**

https://digdeepstandtall.com/ddst-workbook-book-signup

Flashlights and clipboards at the ready.

We're going in.

Your Structural Survey

A Note on Overwhelm:

Before we get started, I want to cover what to do if you feel overwhelmed.

Don't panic! Overwhelm is natural – you're probably overwhelmed because you don't know where to start, but that's actually easy. Remember what we discussed earlier? No matter where you are, there is only one place you can start from and that's where you are *now*. Sounds obvious, but it's true. You can't be anywhere else but here, now.

If you're overwhelmed, you may find grounding techniques helpful. Ground yourself. Look around the room or listen to some of your favourite music. Name countries. Move each part of your body slowly, starting at the top of your head and working down to your toes. Anything that brings you into this moment.

*Warning! If at any point you feel you're actually in danger, seek help immediately. In most countries, this means contacting the emergency services. Many times, I have gone from feeling fine one minute to being triggered in the next. Sometimes I have needed to seek emergency help and there is no shame in this. I don't want you to expect that this is going to happen, but it's good to be prepared. I want you to feel safe.

SURVEY STARTS HERE

To start, find an environment free from distractions where you can be unselfconscious and honest with yourself. That's the only requirement for these exercises.

First impressions

Turn your focus inwards and see what comes to mind. If you're used to doing this, it may feel easy and not very enlightening, but if you've hidden from it, this may be really hard.

By 'turn your focus inwards', I mean to divert your attention from the traffic outside or the hum of the fridge, and see if you can notice what is going on inside. If it helps to close your eyes, go for it. But if not, that's fine. It often helps to take a couple of deep breaths and notice any feelings inside your body.

Below there is a list of questions to work through to help you go deeper.

What first greets you as you look inside?

This is the icebreaker. Self, meet yourself. It's like a speed date. But with yourself. Is that weird? If you've never done this before, it may be eye-opening. Even if you spent loads of time with yourself already, it gives you a snapshot of right now before going into the Blueprint phase.

The prompts are deliberately as random as possible, so you can't get too into your head and formulaic about it.

Don't overthink this. Just write whatever you notice. There's no right or wrong.

Start with point one, and as soon as you can't notice anything else, move to point two, and so on.

If it helps, set a timer for anywhere from 10 minutes to half an hour, whatever feels comfortable – not too long, not too short. If the time runs out and you want to keep going, go for it. Otherwise, stop and move on to the *Your Structural Analysis* section.

1. **Thoughts**: What's the voice in your head saying? What words can you hear? Are they pleasant or uncomfortable? Quiet or incessant?
2. **Feelings**: Do you notice any overriding feelings? Do they feel pleasant or painful? Do you just feel numb and dead, or alive inside?
3. **Ideas**: Do you have ideas about how life should be? What about changes you'd like to make? Or project/business ideas?
4. **Desires**: What do you really want? Don't think, just write it down. There are no right or wrong answers.
5. **Problems**: What bothers you about your life, or self, and needs solving?
6. **Plans**: What are you going to do? Today? Next week? Next year?
7. **Obsessions**: What can't you let go of no matter how hard you try?
8. **Dislikes**: What don't you like about yourself and your life?
9. **Changes**: What changes would you make to your life and self if a genie granted you three magic wishes?
10. **Physical sensations**: What can you feel in your body? Is there tightness, pain? Or do you feel relaxed? Do you feel connected to your body or disconnected?
11. **Trauma**: Be careful with this. Don't go digging. But is there anything you are already aware of that comes from something that hurt you in the past?
12. **Obstacles**: Is there anything that stands in the way of where you want to get to?
13. **Distractions**: What is interrupting this process? Internal and external.
14. **Doubts**: What can't you imagine working or happening?
15. **Self-image concepts**: Who are you, in a sentence? Do you like yourself or want to get as far away from yourself as possible? How would you describe yourself to others?
16. **Inventions**: Have you thought of anything that solves a practical problem? For you, someone else, or the world?
17. **Wild dreams**: What would you do if there were no restrictions, obstacles, or consequences? The sky's the limit.

18. **Fantasies**: What do you imagine that is far-fetched or out of this world?
19. **Questions**: There are no stupid questions. As long as they're genuine, ask away. What do you want to know? What don't you understand?
20. **Addictions**: What do you struggle with that you don't know how to give up?
21. **Worries**: What goes around and around in your head that you're worried about? Is it something you did that you can't take back? Or something that might happen?
22. **Secrets**: What haven't you told others, or what can't you tell people about? (Maybe don't write this one down or write it in code.)
23. **Solutions**: What solves a problem in your life? What can you do to fix something that isn't working?
24. **Fears**: What scares you? What fears get in your way?
25. **Limiting beliefs**: Complete these sentences: "I could never…", "I will only ever be…"
26. **Answers**: What can you answer that you've been wondering? Let the answers come and don't force it. Refer to the questions prompt above and let it flow.

What else do you notice that we haven't already covered?

Great work! Like I said, this may seem simple, but it's actually profound, especially if you have not done this kind of thing before. By keeping it vague and unstructured, it allows your inner self to guide where you're going with it and reveal itself to you. The real power comes from *Your Structural Analysis* coming up now.

Don't worry if you feel you didn't do very well. There's no such thing. As long as you were as honest as you could be and recognised something about yourself, you've succeeded. Even if you couldn't find anything to write, that still tells you something. It means the building is not safe for access yet. That's OK! It will be.

Come back and do this whenever you feel like it, but especially when you've finished reading the book, to see how it has helped with your ability to get to know yourself.

It may be helpful to keep these answers somewhere safe so you can come back and compare (helpfully) and see your progress.

Thanks for taking the time to do this.

Warm up your brain, it's analysis time.

8

ANALYSIS TIME

Complete Your Structural Analysis

Survey complete.

You've just taken a walk around your building and completed your initial survey. You collected as much data as you could. Now, you're either feeling enlightened or thinking your findings look like a complete mess. Either is fine because now we're going to process the data and get some order to it. This will form the basis of *Your 1/5/10 Plan*, which is the tool that will help you turn your dreams into reality. Exciting stuff!

Let's get analysing.

**If you'd like a fillable/printable PDF workbook containing the three exercises
from this book, you can download it here:**

https://digdeepstandtall.com/ddst-workbook-book-signup

ANALYSIS STARTS HERE

Prep

To prepare, take a piece of paper big enough to hold all your findings. Split it into two columns and write 'Above Ground Analysis' and 'Below

Ground Analysis' – one in each column. Alternatively, you can do the same thing, but use separate pieces of paper for each.

Below Ground/Above Ground Analysis

We are going to perform two types of analysis. The first is the Below Ground/Above Ground Analysis. As you now know, the primary aim of this book is to get deeper into the below-ground life. So, we're going to separate your findings out to identify the parts that are the real driving force behind your life. The rest won't go to waste. It will help form the detail of *Your 1/5/10 Plan* outcomes. Also, you're probably more comfortable with the above-ground findings, which is why we're giving them less focus.

Your Analysis

The criteria for this is:

Below Ground is anything that takes place inside you or is inward focussed, like thoughts, feelings, ideas, desires, etc.

Above Ground is anything that takes place outside you or is outwardly focussed, like working out at the gym, relationships, or buying something from the store.

This is not an exact science, and there is overlap. Every aspect of life has both below and above-ground elements to make them work. So, if you think it goes in both columns, put it in both.

Depending on how introverted or extroverted you are, you may have more in one column than another. This is fine.

Just do it quickly, with little thought. And as long as it makes sense to you, it's great.

Once you've done that, you're ready to move on to the next stage. Good ole S.W.O.T.

Prep

If this next step seems like double handling, it's because it is. I've designed it like that deliberately because the aim of the analysis is to turn your random findings into something that you can use to achieve your goals. Doing it this way arrives at a stronger outcome than if it was all done in one go. You might have to trust me on this until you get to the end. The added benefit is that going over the same material in different ways helps to clarify it, organise it, and become more familiar with it.

To prepare, divide two pieces of paper into four so that each piece has a quadrant or square on it. Write: *Above-Ground S.W.O.T Analysis* at the top of one, and *Below-Ground S.W.O.T. Analysis* at the top of the other. Then write **S** in the top left quadrant, **W** in the top right, **O** in the bottom left, and **T** in the bottom right quadrant of each of the two pieces of paper.

Once you've done that, it's analysis time.

Your S.W.O.T. Analysis

Now transfer your Above Ground and Below Ground Analysis into the quadrants on each new sheet. Again, don't worry about getting it perfect. This is for you and your insight only.

I put a lot of thought into what type of analysis to use here, and I decided that this is the most straightforward and powerful. It's simple, easy to get hold of, but also has a lot of depth to it.

S.W.O.T. stands for **S**trengths, **W**eaknesses, **O**pportunities, **T**hreats. Organisations and businesses use it as a strategic planning tool to assess their current position in relation to a project or venture. It works just as well for your life. Traditionally, the strengths and weaknesses are internal and the opportunities and threats, external. For our purposes, we're doing an internal and external version of each.

We're now going to use *Your S.W.O.T Analysis* to further break down your findings from earlier on. If more areas come to mind that you didn't think of during *Your Structural Survey*, you can add them in as you go along.

Below Ground
S - Your strengths are your greatest assets: e.g. courage, intuition, dreams, intellect.
W - Your weaknesses are the areas you may need help in or to learn more about: e.g. lack of confidence, rage, lethargy, judging others.
O - Your opportunities are the resources available to you to further your cause: e.g. a good sense of what will become a niche market, a new willingness to try something outside your comfort zone, a newfound energy for life.
T - Your threats are things to insure and protect against: e.g. self-sabotage, resistance to change, addictions, crippling fears.

Above Ground:
S - Your strengths are your greatest assets: e.g. people skills, good money management, a flair for DIY, physical fitness.
W - Your weaknesses are the areas you may need help in or you may need to do some serious learning: e.g. time management, tidiness, listening while others are talking, trying new things.
O - Your opportunities are the resources available to you to further your cause: e.g. a wealthy investor who has taken a shine to you, falling house prices, a course that will give you the skill you need to take the next step towards your dream, an invitation to join a prestigious club.
T - Your threats are things to insure and protect against: e.g. stock market decline, a neighbour that has it in for you, marital troubles, growing credit card debt.

Spend some time looking over what you've just produced. What do you notice? Hopefully, you'll see how all those random findings you gathered in *Your Structural Survey* actually have a direct impact on your life and goals.

If it helps, make notes on what it tells you about your life and your current position.

That's your survey complete. I hope it was helpful.

As we move on to the Blueprint section, which deals with where you want to end up, you can do it knowing that you have an idea of where you are right now. This makes the whole process clearer.

Keep the final analysis nearby because we're going to draw on it alongside *Your 1/5/10 Plan,* which we'll come to at the end of the next section. This is where you'll decide all the elements of your superstructure and draw up the plans for how to build it.

Put on your architect hat and sharpen your pencil.

It's time to get those creative juices flowing.

BLUEPRINTS

9

SET YOUR INNER CHILD FREE

Embrace Your Role as Architect in the Process

You stand and stare.

And, for the first time, you see what you've been hiding from.

The whole place is a mess. Stuff everywhere.

There're massive cracks. And bits crumbling before your eyes.

You wonder, "How can this be my life?"

"How do other people have it so easy?"

It's hard, but this time, you refuse to look away, and you notice more that you'd long forgotten or lost touch with. Memories you'd locked away. Habits you'd ignored. Personality traits you wish you didn't have. And feelings that you'd rather never have to face up to.

But as you continue to take stock, you see beyond all that and ideas begin to flow.

You imagine again what life could be like if you can catch a break.

But how?

How do you go from where you are now to where you want to be?

Awaken Your Inner Architect

Inside you is an architect. A capable designer that can envisage infinite possibilities to realise your vision of a limitless life.

Learning to tap into the architect role is easier than it may first appear. It is really just a case of connecting with your inner child and letting your imagination run wild.

There are many people who have already mastered the process we're talking about here. So, we can look to them for guidance.

Many of these people got to where they are because life gave them a good start. There *are* lessons to be learnt from these people, but since we can't replicate their position, a lot of the lessons may not help directly.

There is one lesson we can learn from anyone, regardless of their start in life, and that is this: anyone who is living their dream life has learnt the role of architect to some extent. They have designed a plan that guides their daily decisions and shows them what to focus on. This is true, regardless of whether they are aware of it.

They may have learnt it unconsciously from parents or caregivers that instilled it in them as a way of life, or they may have learnt it the hard way. Either way, they learnt the skills to design a plan and execute it.

For many people, this isn't something concrete and clear, like the plan we're going to create here. It's more like a picture they have inside them – a beacon guiding them home. They couldn't explain to anyone else how they have achieved what they have. They just had a sense of what they wanted and made it happen.

Your plan is going to be as concrete as it needs to be to ensure success. It's going to take the mystery out of why your life has been the way it has.

Your 1/5/10 Plan is the blueprint for your dream superstructure. I'll explain what it is soon.

Your Dream Superstructure

In your role as architect, you are going to produce the detailed drawings that will represent every square inch of your dream life. If that feels too much like hard work, a simple sketch on the back of a napkin will do. But, if there's any area where it's exciting to get into the nitty-gritty and get specific, it's this. Think about it. You are designing your dream life and you get to decide every aspect. It could be big and exciting, it could be cosy and peaceful, it could be a combination of the two and everything in between.

Now, if the word superstructure makes you think about high-rise office buildings in smog-filled cities, you can replace it with the word mansion instead. Or whatever works for you. I've chosen superstructure because of the heights they reach. Visualise what brings you joy and call it whatever you want. Just allow it to be limitless in your mind's eye. And make sure you like what you're seeing.

As you relax into this process, you will see you already have everything it takes to make it through. And once you've eliminated all the unnecessary clutter, it really is quite simple.

1. Get in touch with your inner self ✓
2. See where you are right now ✓
3. Discover what lights you up and brings you joy
4. Make a plan to get there
5. Execute
6. Repeat

One thing I highly recommend is to find physical/digital pictures that capture what you want your life to look like. You can cut pictures out of magazines, save them from the internet, or use Pinterest to create a vision board. Clare and I did this at the beginning of our relationship, and when we look back at that board, we can see that what we've wanted has changed little. The pictures have grown and developed, but at the heart, they are the same as when we first thought of them.

You may find it helpful to find a picture of an actual building that has a feeling similar to how you want your life to feel. But this could also get confusing because we're not really talking about a physical building, even though your dream home will probably appear in your plan. Whatever you decide, it just needs to work for you – to give you something to look at which represents your goals and dreams. This is especially helpful in those dark times when you can lose all perspective and forget what you're working towards.

When I started designing my life, my dreams felt like impossible wishes that everyone, including me, knew could never really happen. Then over the years, the possibility grew and a point came where I had thought about and gone over them so many times that they were real on the inside of me. For years, I have seen myself as an entrepreneur, despite not having any business success. But that fact doesn't touch the reality on the inside of me.

When I was homeless and literally lying in the gutter, I still couldn't shake the image of my dream life and who I really was. When Clare and I were living in a hostel with people setting off the fire alarms with their crack pipes, I still had on the inside of me the image of our Georgian detached house on the outskirts of Bath. Those dreams got me through my worst years.

I lived in one small town for a few years, on and off. I used to have conversations with people who talked as though there was a law stating that they must never leave the town on pain of death. They clearly believed that town was their lot and there was nothing they could do about it. I'd be sitting there in the local pub, sinking drink after drink, far more wasted than them, with no job and no prospects. On the surface, they would seem in a much better place than me, but I would blow their minds with my ideas and ambitions to make something of myself.

I'm not saying these things to big myself up. I'm saying that no matter what state your life is in right now, or in the years to come, you can still hold on to that vision – your architect's drawings that represent your dream superstructure. And, when the first row of bricks is in place, at that moment, the years or decades of toil and hardship will melt away, and you won't think about them anymore.

Sounds good, doesn't it?

Only you can be the architect of your life. Start drawing up your plans now and never give up that privilege again.

You'll never regret it!

Planning is Fun

"Right, let's have a planning meeting at 8 am on Monday morning to discuss team morale and the way we can improve our upsell strategy to get more conversions in our customer-facing roles." Blah, blah, blah!

That kind of planning is mind-numbing, soul-destroying, life-sucking drudgery. What we're talking about is playing, like you did way back when. Remember the way you could turn anything into something else, like a table into a cave, or a big stick into a laser gun? That inner child is still there, waiting to inspire new imaginations.

This is not corporate planning, this is life planning, and there will be times when you feel you could burst with the ideas that come to you, especially when you recover dreams you thought you'd lost. You never really forgot them. You just buried them because you didn't know you were allowed to hold on to them. And, you didn't yet realise it is your privilege and right to make them happen because it's your life and nobody else's.

As the saying goes; if you fail to plan, you plan to fail. Plan your life for success.

Personal Flair

What type of architect do you think you are? Are you a maximalist, or do you like sparse, zen-like spaces? Are you all business and formality, or do you really like spontaneity and randomness?

As we go into the next chapter, I want you to allow your hidden flair to surface. Don't be afraid to let it shine. Remember, nothing is permanent in this process. You can reassess or change your mind at any point.

Inject as much of your personality into your designs as you can. They are just for you.

10

THE SKY REALLY IS THE LIMIT
Dare to Dream Like a Child Again

But that's a massive risk, isn't it?

What if it ends in disappointment? Again.

Your life might bore you right now, but at least it's safe. You can live with that.

But things keep reminding you of your dream. You're out for a meal with friends and they talk about the adventure they've been on in South America. And there's that advert on the TV that keeps telling you to dream bigger.

It's inspiring. But thoughts of failure are just too painful. And you mustn't let yourself forget the last hare-brained scheme you left your job for, which fizzled out after a few weeks, leaving you unemployed and depressed. That's where dreaming gets you.

Your mind is made up. You'll play it safe. That's the responsible thing to do.

But every night as you're drifting off, those dreams come alive again.

And you want them so badly.

So, what do you do?

Take __ALL__ the Limits off of Life

The thing is, playing it safe and denying your dreams leads to certainty. The certainty that things will stay the same and that everything you hope for remains a distant fantasy – a dream of the 'pipe' variety.[13] Certainty

---

[13] 'Pipe Dream' Definition: 1. an Idea or Plan That Is Impossible or Very Unlikely to Happen: 2. an Idea or Plan That Is Not Practical or Possible. Cambridge Advanced Learner's Dictionary & Thesaurus, Cambridge University Press, "pipe dream," dictionary.cambridge.org/dictionary/english/pipe-dream.

is the enemy of possibility. So, if you want access to all the possibilities in the universe, you'll need to take *all* the limits off.

As with everything, you'll need to start small and build up, but that doesn't mean you can't *intend* to take all the limits off right now. You don't even need to know how. You can resolve in yourself that you will no longer live a life that is constrained by limitations based on fear and false views of yourself.

This may feel scary, but I promise you it's worth it.

One thing to watch out for is the backlash that can occur in the wake of an intention like that. A voice on the radio saying, "Now is not the time to leave your job and start a business. The economy is too unstable." Or someone you'd forgotten about popping up on your social media just to persuade you out of your newfound enthusiasm for life.

These occurrences are one of two things. Either, they would have happened anyway, but you notice them because they challenge you, or it is a direct attack because you are challenging other people's limits and they don't like it.

Limits feel safe because they make us feel in control. But that safety can quickly become stifling. Commit today to taking the limits off and setting your life free.

What are Dreams Worth?

Dreams are your starting place. They are full of hope. The hope that things can change. And they fulfil your potential.

It is said that ideas are worthless, and execution is everything. By this token, dreams would be worthless too because they are just ideas. But that statement is an above-ground statement, and it's incomplete. Dreams alone will not get things done above ground, but they can motivate an army of people. Think Martin Luther-King Jr's dream. I've

71

heard no one call that a worthless dream. Because it helped to spark the civil rights movement, changing the course of history and making the world a better place. So, even above ground, ideas and dreams are not worthless.

Below ground, dreams are pure gold. They are one of the most valuable things you possess. They are an integral part of your foundation, which you can build on for the rest of your life.

When I first started this process, dreaming hurt my brain and brought up so much pain, it felt unbearable. In time, imagining bigger and bigger things, I eventually got to where there is nothing I can't imagine.

I spent many years mostly in bed because of chronic pain and fatigue. This gave me the opportunity to dream to my heart's content. As I mentioned, I actually got to a point where what I was dreaming was so real that I felt like I was there already, so I stayed there as long as I could. Life always brought me back at some point and the good feelings wore off, giving me a rude awakening. I gradually realised that having dreams would never satisfy me if I did nothing about them. This is not the aim here. I want you to get there.

I have a picture hanging on the wall in my living room of a crescent Earth rising in the lunar sky. The image is from a photo taken by NASA astronauts in 1972 from Apollo 17. It is on the front of a greeting card given to me by my brother-in-law when I left the youth work charity he runs. It is such a special picture because it offers a unique perspective on the earth and its position in the universe.

The inscription inside is inspired by a Robert F. Kennedy speech. The inscription in the card says:

"There are those that look at things the way they are, and ask why?
I dream of things that haven't been revealed yet, and ask why not?"[14]

The card is a constant reminder to me to look for the parts of life that I haven't yet discovered and keep an open mind.

I wrote a song with my brother, Al, called 'Sweet Little Butterfly'. It's based around someone on their way to work who's stuck in a traffic jam, caught up in the same old same old. The heart of the song is an invitation for everyone who feels stuck to dare to dream of a different life. The chorus ends with, "Let your imagination run wild". And that's my invitation to you today.

You can listen to *Sweet Little Butterfly* here:

https://digdeepstandtall.com/music/sweet-little-butterfly

Dare to dream your wildest dreams. And your future self will thank your current self mightily.

---

[14] jfklibrary.org. 'Remarks at the University of Kansas, March 18, 1968 | JFK Library'. John F. Kennedy Presidential Library and Museum, www.jfklibrary.org/learn/about-jfk/the-kennedy-family/robert-f-kennedy/robert-f-kennedy-speeches/remarks-at-the-university-of-kansas-march-18-1968. Accessed 25 November, 2021.

11

NO GREATER MOTIVATION
Your 'Why' is Your Reason for Everything

You're busy doing life.

It rolls from one day to the next.

It's full. But it never seems to satisfy.

You've got good friends and you're moving up on your chosen career path.

But is that really enough?

You've achieved some major milestones and ticked off some bucket list items.

But deep down, you know those things are more about your social media feed, to impress other people. They're not for you.

Even the parts of your life that really are *you* don't feel quite right somehow. You hear other people talk about their passions and think, "I want what they've got." They seem animated and alive. Almost driven.

But what is it that gives them their spark?

And what will give you yours?

Your WHY.

Your WHY is part of your deepest foundation. It is your reason for being. Your motivation. And the driving force behind the greatest expression of who you are.

I first learnt about my WHY from Simon Sinek in his books, *Start With WHY and Find Your WHY*. I know of nothing else like it and highly recommend both of them.

On his website, he says,

"The WHY is the purpose, cause or belief that drives every one of us."[15]

In his books, he helps the reader to visualise what their WHY is with a picture of three concentric circles. You have your WHY in the centre, your HOW in the second ring, and your WHAT in the outer ring.

The opening scenario in this section portrays a life full of WHATS with some understanding of the HOWS. Without the WHY, it's not possible to know whether the WHAT you're doing is what you really want to be doing. It's just going through the motions, trying to do what's expected based on what we see in other people's lives, or their expectations of us.

There are people at the top of their game that you may envy who are a million miles from where they want to be because they don't know their WHY. They may be more successful than you in a lot of ways, but that doesn't mean they are more fulfilled.

The WHY books take you through a process, much like this book, that arrives at a connection with who you really are. At the end of the process, you produce your WHY statement.

Here's mine:

To encourage people to push the bounds of creativity so that they can join the adventure of life.

I hope you can see how this fits with my aim for this book. Before reading Simon Sinek's WHY books, I had very little connection with the concepts

---

[15] Simon Sinek. "Find Your WHY." Simon Sinek, Simon Sinek Inc. Accessed 25 Nov. 2021. simonsinek.com/find-your-why.

in that statement. Once I got hold of it, it propelled me towards a different life that has led me to writing a book of my own.

The HOWS in the second ring are *how* you do your *why*.

Here are my HOWS:

Get to the heart
Keep looking until you find what really matters

Take inspired risks
Choose the path that most excites you

Maximise potential
Live life to the full in each moment

Live free
Remove all limitations so you are truly free to choose

Discover new ways of seeing
Always be learning and never settle for the way things appear to be

Again, I hope you can see how this resonates with what you know of me so far. Every time I read it back, it just makes perfect sense to me. Everything I do now is an attempt to be more and more in line with these statements. I forget them often, and then when I'm reminded of them, they always get me back on course.

The interesting thing is, the WHAT isn't as important as we've been led to believe. When you know your WHY and HOWS, the WHATS reveal themselves effortlessly.

Remember the time when you had to choose which subjects to study in school? Or meeting with the career advisor? If you were like me, you didn't really have a clue. The amazing thing is when your WHY and HOWS are clear, you can do any WHAT that is in harmony with them.

As you've seen, my WHY and HOWS are adventure and ideas-based. They make sense of why I'm not drawn to office jobs and could never stick them out. I value freedom too much. So, what's a better option? As long as I am hitting my WHY and most of the HOW points, I am free to do whatever is in me to do.

There is no quick and easy shortcut to finding your WHY. You must do the work. If this intrigues you, invest in *Start With Why* and, if that speaks to you, also *Find Your Why*.

Buy *Start With Why* here:

https://www.digdeepstandtall.com/get-start-with-why-book
(Affiliate link)

If you skip this bit, it's not the end of the world, so don't worry. The rest will still be helpful.

Knowing your WHY will give you confidence about all your HOWS and WHATS.

Without it, you may just be guessing.

12

THE KEY TO REALISING YOUR DREAM LIFE
Your 1/5/10 Plan

'How did I get here?' you ask.

It's far from where you'd imagined ending up in the days before life got serious.

You remember believing you'd go places and make a difference in the world.

You imagined yourself doing only the things you loved, surrounded by people that inspired you, and enjoying every minute.

What went wrong?

It's not like you haven't tried. You're always looking for ways to escape. You just haven't nailed it yet.

There's that motivational course you spent hundreds on to beat procrastination. You'll get around to that soon.

And you're always thinking about new business ideas. You just haven't found *the one* yet.

You know you need to get organised about it, but you're not sure where to start.

You don't have any sort of plan.

Well, that stops now.

The Simplest Plan is The Best Plan

"If you don't know where you're going, any road will get you there."[16]

---

[16] Donna Tinberg. "Lessons from the Cheshire Cat." Education Resources Information Center, ERIC, September 2012, 2021. eric.ed.gov/?id=EJ997652.

If you search the web for planning methods, it may quickly overwhelm you. Each method has its merits, but the best plan of all is the simplest plan of all. Because it is the one most likely to get you to your destination.

'Simple' doesn't mean lacking detail. The simple part refers to the creation of the plan – how quickly and easily you can create and execute it.

Planning is not a one-time thing. You need to reassess en route and remain flexible until you know you've established a destination worth heading for. Even then, there will still be tweaks along the way.

Enough talk about plans.

Let's get yours going.

Your 1/5/10 Plan

**If you'd like a fillable/printable PDF workbook containing the three exercises
from this book, you can download it here:**

https://digdeepstandtall.com/ddst-workbook-book-signup

Your 1/5/10 Plan is a time-bound plan, which is what makes it powerful. It starts with the end in mind and works backwards to give you specific actions to perform today to get you progressively nearer to your goal.

Prep

Take four pieces of paper and write '10-Year Plan' on one piece, and 'Five-Year Plan' on the next, 'One-Year Plan' on the next, and 'One-Month Plan' on the last piece. Alternatively, you can do this on a laptop or whiteboard. If you do it on the whiteboard, don't forget to take a picture of each plan before rubbing it out. You're going to need to look at each part of the process.

PLAN STARTS HERE

Your 10-Year Plan

Answer these questions in as much detail as you can:

1. Where do you want to be 10 years from now?

This is where *taking all the limits off* comes into play. A decade is a long time. It's more than enough time to achieve even your wildest dreams. You don't have to know at this point how you are going to achieve them. That comes later. For now, it's securing them in written form, so you have something to work from and refer to. The 10-year goals are the hardest part because you're starting from scratch. It gets easier.

2. Where do you want to be five years from now?

Next, you repeat the process for five years, basing it on the 10-year goals you've just written. The idea is to establish where you need to reach by the halfway point (five years) in order to make it to your 10-year goal.

3. Where do you want to be one year from now?

You then repeat the same process for a year's time. This is the point where it starts to feel within reach. It's not so *out there* anymore because the major goal has been broken down and made achievable.

4. Where do you want to be one month from now?

Finally, you decide on your goals for the next month. These are the things you will begin actioning immediately to take the first steps towards your dream life.

And that's it.

See how simple that was?

Decide Your Priority Goal

Now you've got all your goals down, you need to identify your priority goal. This is the goal that you will give your focus and energy to. The one that you'd choose if you were granted just one wish. Your priority.

There is no such thing as 'priorities', at least there never used to be. It's only our modern culture complicating things to fit more in. We can only really give our full attention to one thing at a time, and that's true here. For Clare and I, that's our money goal right now because that goal unlocks so many other things we want to achieve.

There's no issue with having other goals in the mix (although, I recommended only three or four at a time), but when it comes down to either/or choices, you'll know ahead of time which goal is going to get your attention.

Highlight that priority goal now.

Crack Open Your Analysis

Now you've laid out your goals, it's time to make use of *Your Structural Analysis*. Your organised findings will help to form a solid foundation for your goals.

Next, I want you to match *Your S.W.O.T Analysis* findings to your 10-year goals. For each goal, write down the relevant **S**trengths, **W**eaknesses, **O**pportunities, and **T**hreats. You may need to start another piece of paper to organise this and make it neater.

A *Strength* example: if your first strength is *writing skills*, and your first goal is *start a blog*, that's clearly relevant, but if your first goal is *12% body fat*, it's unlikely you will match writing skills to it. But you decide what's best for you.

A **Weakness** example: If your first weakness is *fear of spiders* and your first goal is *buy dream house*, then whether it's relevant will depend on your location. If your dream house is in the UK, then it probably isn't a match. But, if it's Nicaragua or Australia, maybe so.

Once you've completed this process, you'll have the full picture – where you are now to 10 years into the future, living your dream life.

BONUS EXERCISE: S.M.A.R.T Goals

S.M.A.R.T stands for **S**pecific, **M**easurable, **A**chievable, **R**elevant, and **T**ime-based.
Whereas a general goal is something like 'Spend more time with the kids' (which is vague and hard to keep to), a S.M.A.R.T goal would look something like this:

(**S**) I will free up an hour a day to spend with the kids, (**M**) three days a week, (**A**) on weekends and my least busy workday, (**R**) which helps to achieve my priority goal of spending more time with the family. (**T**) I'll start tomorrow.

To break down your month goals into actionable steps, I recommend turning them into S.M.A.R.T Goals to leave little room for uncertainty or failure.

You can then break those down even further into specific *to-dos* to be actioned throughout the month. You'll find everything you need to expand on what I've given you here online or in relevant books.

But this book isn't really about all that above-ground stuff. It's about digging deep to stand tall.

So, let's get back below ground and look at the skills that are going to help you build your superstructure.

SKILLS

13

YOUR GREATEST SKILL FOR SUCCESS
Never Stop Learning

Remember being born?

Thought not.

It went something like this:

After months of just being, and having everything you needed, you entered the world without your consent. Suddenly, you're in this crazy space full of bright lights, deafening sounds, and a flood of emotions and sensations you've never experienced. You open your mouth and let out a cry – oh, the pain.

From the very first moment, you are learning with every part of your being.

In time, you begin to make sense of it all. That's my mum, that's a cloud, I like peanut butter, I don't like sprouts. I need my nappy changed, I mustn't go in that cupboard...

And so, the endless stream of learning continues second by second.

You also learn to imagine what you could become – I want to be a firefighter or a ballet dancer or help people who are unhappy.

Before long, it's time for school. Where you learn, but differently from before. And gradually, rote learning and praise for ability to recall facts replaces your in-built ways of learning. Instead of fascination for every part of life, you are now obsessed and anxious with scoring 75/100 in your next test because that somehow proves you are worth something.

And so, learning becomes a dirty word and loses its appeal. Stuck in a classroom day after endless day, learning things that take you years to discover have little application in the real world. Things like, 'How do I open a bank account and withdraw money?' 'How do I balance household chores?' 'Which job should you go for when you have multiple offers?' 'How can you tell if a person is trustworthy or not?' 'How do you balance the workload in your job and deal with a manager who is intent on putting more and more on you?'

By the time you're done with formal education, you are glad to see the back of learning. Now you can just get on with living and enjoying life.

Until the day you realise there's a lot you don't know that you need to.

What can you do about that?

Remember How to Really Learn

Your experience may not have been as extreme as the opening example. But you'll have lost some of the joy of learning about the world around you, purely for the sake of it.

Our first skill in this digging deep adventure is 'learning' – because, without it, you are going to stay exactly where you are.

No matter how far you've strayed, you can learn to love learning again.

It will gradually come back as you connect with your inner child and set your imagination free.

Remembering how to learn starts with recovering inquisitiveness and fascination.

You're Not Stupid for Not Knowing

Would you call someone stupid if they joined in on a game you were playing and they, having never played it before, asked what the rules are? Probably not, right? But that's what we've all experienced in life – being ridiculed for lack of knowledge.

When we are born, we don't have a clue about anything and we have to learn it all from the people and environment around us. If people care for us, and our surroundings are peaceful and supportive, we are likely to thrive and learn what we need to grow up and stand on our own two feet. If people fail us and the environment is hostile, we are likely to suffer and, as a result, fail to thrive and learn what we need to survive.

It's very hard to imagine what someone else knows and what they don't. I think part of the human condition is looking at other people and assuming they know what we know because it's just obvious to us. But each life is so different and with it, each person's deep-seated beliefs. Maybe life taught you it's 'every person for themselves' and 'don't trust anyone'. Or, maybe it's "Do unto others as you would have them do to you." And "To give is better than to receive." These learned beliefs will have wildly different consequences and outcomes.

A hard point in my journey of self-discovery, which I still struggle with today, was realising that there are certain things that I missed out on in my developmental years. This is not something that is visible to other people. It mostly affects my ability to learn and process certain things, making it harder for me to get hold of what others find straightforward. One example of this is emotions. I still really struggle to connect with and know what it is I'm feeling. Sometimes, it takes Clare recognising it for me to have a clue at all.

The hard thing about this is, I don't get to skip that bit of learning because I'm now an adult. Not if I really want to live a full and enjoyable life. I still have to learn some skills that other people learnt decades ago when they were taking their first steps. That's humbling and sometimes humiliating. It's made harder because I've learnt ways of covering up and hiding the parts that are undeveloped, so there's no external pressure to do anything about them. Unless I'm in a crisis, nobody would see anything but a capable adult who has it together.

I'm finding it uncomfortable to admit these things because part of me still wants you to see me as the persona that I've perfected and put forward to the world for so many years.

If you can relate to any of this, you know how hard it feels.

If you can learn to feel comfortable with where you really are in your learning process, you will give your dreams a much greater chance of success. Remember that Marie Forleo quote from earlier, "Everything is figureoutable"? Well, that's only true if you will admit you don't know something.

Albert Einstein is often credited as saying it like this:

"The more I learn, the more I realize how much I don't know."[17]

I've heard he was a pretty clever guy, so it's worth considering what he has to say about this, don't you think?

Remain humble and admit what you don't know, starting now.

Learn to Learn

Learning is truly the greatest skill you can master. Why? Because it is the starting point for everything that depends on you. It's where we started our lives in the first place and if we return to that state, our lives can get back the transformation that was a normal, everyday occurrence when we were young.

The beauty is that no matter where you are now, no matter what you don't know, you can learn it. All of it!

And, all lasting change comes from learning because it originates in the deep parts of us, below ground. So, if you hold on to your safe beliefs about yourself, others, and the world around you, you're probably staying right where you are. But, if you open yourself up to seeing life

---

[17] James Rouw. "The More I Don't Know, the More I Want to Learn." Nu Squared, 2014, 2021. www.nusquared.com/blog/the-more-i-dont-know-the-more-i-want-to-learn.

with fresh eyes, you'll soon find that things that got stuck for years or decades can change in a heartbeat.

I dissociated through all my years at school because I hated every second and couldn't cope with how I felt inside. When I left, I immediately discovered my love of learning, for myself, again. I got on the internet and began asking questions about everything. Not only trivial subjects that interested me but also deeper things like, "How do you learn?" And, "How do you know when to trust people?" I read books for the first time in years and got to where I was reading 100+ books a year.

My brain had been so switched off to the world around me and the processes of learning that learning again for the first time actually hurt. It was like the cogs had become seized and, as they sprang into action again, they were grinding against each other. Gradually, it became natural again to be inquisitive and to absorb more and more information. Now, I have to hold myself back because I could learn about everything and anything all day long.

Being raised in a nurturing environment, we naturally learn things that seem to happen almost automatically. But if we don't get that nurturing, we are not then exempt from learning those things. Like my mum, you still have to learn it even if you're 76. And it can be a lot harder to grasp by that point, and that's a great reason to start now. Don't delay!

The Issue of Memory

Memory is a big issue for many people. But everyone can learn to remember more with one simple change that really works.

It's this:

You remember what you are interested in… that's it!

What do you remember most easily in life? People's names? Types of birds? Pi to 100 numbers? If you think about the things you remember, it's because you have a genuine interest in that thing. So, if you want to remember something you've previously struggled with, you just have to find out how you can be genuinely interested in that thing.

The way to become interested in something is to find what it is about that thing that benefits you. You may remember everyone's faces because people fascinate you, but get nobody's names right. But, if you pay attention to people's names, they all have a quality about them. Some are plain and common and some seem ridiculous. Also, using people's names in the right way (not overusing for the sake of it) makes them feel you are interested in them. Which helps to form bonds and strengthen relationships.

In the same way, let's say you keep coming across people talking about discipline and realise this is something you need to learn. Even if you have no prior interest in discipline and have found it boring, you can become instantly interested in it by asking, "What can discipline give me that I can't have without it?" You can then discover that it frees up hours in the day for you to chill or do the thing that most lights you up. And, if you're a people person, you can learn from people who have led a disciplined life with all the fascinating details about them interspersed.

It's possible to make the most initially boring things in the world into things you become completely fascinated with. And you'll have a hard time forgetting anything you're completely fascinated with.

This is the secret of memory.

Accumulation of Skills

We're focussing on below-ground stuff here, but this principle also applies above ground.

Learning to learn is like learning to use muscles again after years of inactivity. At first, it is pure effort and, like I said before, can actually hurt. It takes everything in you to stay with it, and it feels like there's no room for anything else. But, in time, the thing you're learning becomes subconsciously embedded and you no longer have to think about it all the time. When it gets to that point, it's almost effortless. It's just in you. Then you can learn the next thing, and the next. There comes a point when you no longer need to limit yourself to just one thing at a time and you can learn multiple things in one go because you've built up your tolerance. That's when things get exciting.

So, if you're just getting started on yourself, take it one step at a time and try not to get frustrated with your progress. 1. Change one thing only. 2. Repeat. I promise your capacity for learning will increase in time and things will feel easier.

In psychological terms, the law of repetition is a theory that learning increases with the repetition of a process

Information alone won't get you to where you want to be, but once it's established in your head and heart, it can help form your core beliefs and values, and that's when the lasting change happens.

No matter the upbringing you've had or the quality of the life-education you've received, there is one teacher that you can rely on. Yourself. It's great if you can surround yourself with people wiser than you who have already built the life that you dream of. But waiting for those people might mean the death of your dreams. So, instead, learn to learn and learn to teach yourself. I promise you won't regret it!

The Tunnel of Progress

As we talked about earlier, learning is a progressive process. When we first encounter a subject, there are so many possibilities and we have not yet established our position in relation to that subject.

So, how do we get from this position of uncertainty to a place of clarity? I picture this process as the journey through a long tunnel.

As we enter the tunnel, it is wide enough to accommodate whatever we carry with us, with no limits on what we can carry. In learning terms, we don't yet know what is important or what resonates with us about a certain subject, so we keep hold of anything that could be useful.

As we move on towards the centre of the tunnel, it narrows, forcing us to shed some of what we're carrying. This is the time where we are getting to grips with our personal preferences and forming our worldview on that subject. We throw out what we don't need along the way.

At the centre, the tunnel is only wide enough to fit us through, plus one item, so we must settle on one thing to take with us. This feels almost like certainty because we have selected one concept or piece of information over the many that we have a preference for or are choosing to believe.

As we move on from the centre of the tunnel, there is room to carry more again. Having settled on the one option – our benchmark – we have something to assess all other options by, which then helps us to be more selective about the many possibilities available to us.

We eventually leave the tunnel for a wide-open space. With our benchmark established, we can expand our horizons and try new things. From this point on, we will always have something to compare new information or ideas to so we can assess what to do with them.

For me, a practical example of this is reading. After years of having forgotten that I enjoyed reading, I started reading novels but would so often be disappointed because I had no criteria for what to read. I didn't know what I liked and didn't. One day, my friend, George, recommended the Jack Reacher series by Lee Child and I was instantly hooked. It was exactly what I'd been looking for but didn't know it.

From that point on, I had a benchmark for the style of novel that I was looking for. After I'd finished all the current Jack Reacher books, it wasn't long before I'd found the Rapp series by Vince Flynn, which has a similar style, and again, I was sold. I'd found my benchmark and orientated myself to what is most *me*. After this, when I tried books by new authors, I now found I could enjoy them in a way that I couldn't before because I had found that all-important first one. If I'd come across those books before, I would have probably dismissed them because I was in search of my benchmark and knew they weren't it.

This process will take you on a journey through the tunnel of progress and help you narrow down the millions of possibilities to find what is most *you*. And your world will become a wide-open space for you to explore.

Unlearning

The learning process is not just about learning. It is equally about unlearning as well.

For example, if your parents taught you as a child not to trust anyone because of the things they had suffered at the hands of other people, you will need to unlearn some of this in order to have the life you want. You cannot hold the view that no one is trustworthy and also have good relationships with others. This is something that I've had to work really hard on, especially with my family and Clare because I didn't have any proof that it was safe to trust anybody. Even the very people whose job it was to protect and care for me had failed me, so why would anyone else do better?

As I dared to trust, people showed themselves as trustworthy. Some of them were people I didn't expect this from. As I made sense of my childhood and could talk things through with my mum, a different picture of my upbringing came into view and I could see things through the eyes of an adult as opposed to a traumatised child.

I came to see that, overall, my mum was giving everything she had for me and my siblings. But she had never learnt how to take care of herself, so she didn't know how to best care for us. She was always so exhausted that she had little left to give us. As I understood these things,

I could see that I *could* trust her. And, after that, I saw that many of my best traits are down to her tenacity and her unwillingness to just accept things the way they are. Growing up, she was the one who most showed the attitude of striving to learn and push for more.

If I hadn't challenged my viewpoints and been willing to learn, I wouldn't have the relationship I have with my mum today.

If you think you know everything already, you can learn nothing new. For many years now, I have tried not to be concerned with how much I know. Instead, I get excited about all there is to learn. Now, I can learn from almost any source or person. My nephews, when they were still young, taught me a lot and if they pointed something out in me that was not right, I did my best to be humble and accept it. Not because I'm a saint. But because if you aren't learning, then you aren't growing. And if you aren't growing, then you can't reach the place where you can stand strong.

Learning is hard. Unlearning is harder because you are dealing with something that is already established and deeply ingrained. It feels comfortable to stay in that place because it's familiar and settled. But, if you want to reach your dream life, you've got to get those gears turning in the other direction and learn, learn, learn.

14

WHEN YOUR PARADIGM SHIFTS

Defining Moments When Your Worldview Changes Forever

You're lying in bed.

Pretending to be asleep.

Trying not to fall asleep at the same time.

Ages pass and you think, "I'm sure he's normally here by now. Where is he?"

Then, suddenly, the door creaks and you lay as still as you can. You risk a peek because there's no light except the glow of the night light in the corner.

The bearded man sneaks across the floorboards with his sack in hand to the end of your bed. His white beard appears yellow in the light and you see his enormous belly under the red and white wool coat.

As he attaches the sack to the end of your bed, something falls out onto his foot.

"Damn it!" he cries.

"Daddy, what are you doing here? Where's Santa?"

"What do you mean 'Daddy'?" he asks in the bellowing *ho, ho, ho* voice you'd expect. But, then you put your bedside lamp on and the first thing you notice is the black wiry beard poking out from behind the white. And something that looks a bit like string coming from above his ears.

"Daddy, I know it's you," you say.

That's when it all unravels. He sits you down and has *the talk* with you.

"Santa isn't real, son. It was always me in a costume."

Your paradigm has well and truly shifted. Forever.

Perception vs. Reality

As we talked about in the last chapter, you've learnt a lot about what you believe and what you value from the world around you, especially your parents. Your worldview is largely a result of where you were born, in what time, and who the people were that surrounded you. Aspects of that view are great and have contributed to the best bits of who you are today. Some of it is just rubbish.

In order to build your life successfully, there will need to be several paradigm shifts in that worldview so that you can form a new view that is in line with your own heart and values. Some of these shifts will take years and some will be like giving birth (so I'm told). The reason being that you cannot successfully hold opposing ideas and expect a single outcome. The result will be confusion.

Perception never automatically equals reality, no matter how real it seems. But our perception always gives us our sense of reality. This then dictates or colours our experience.

One of our lifelong jobs is to check our perceptions and make sure they match up with reality. This is not straightforward because nobody can agree on what reality actually is. However, you must decide for yourself since no one else can decide it for you.

A very simple picture of the problem of perception vs. reality is how easy it is to get lost while navigating a jungle. You can be absolutely certain you are walking in a straight line (perception) and find yourself back in the same place a couple of hours later (reality). It happened to me on a walk with my brother and it blew my mind. I thought it only happened in films.

There are many people in the world who speak with certainty and will persuade anyone who doesn't hold their view of 'the truth' to come around to their way. These people are everywhere and will pounce on you at the first hint that you are challenging one of their sacred cows.

Let them have their 'truth', and you find yours. What they perceive and believe is of no value to you and your life, and vice versa. They may not be interested in lasting change and wild dreams anyway. So, don't pay them too much attention.

Logical fallacies are a trap that people fall into easily unless they have learnt about them. One example of this is 'argument to authority', which means that you believe something *because* the person saying it is an authority figure – doctor, millionaire, pastor – then that makes it true. This is a logical fallacy because it is NEVER true just because someone in authority says it. Even though a doctor is statistically more likely to tell you what you need to know about your health, they can also give poor advice, while an untrained child could diagnose your illness because they recognise the symptoms.

By learning about a fallacy once, you can avoid many pitfalls in understanding for the rest of your life.

For more examples, check out https://yourlogicalfallacyis.com.

Some of the worst unreality-based perceptions I faced are the fear-based kind. Many refer to these as 'paper tigers' because a paper tiger may look scary, but it can't hurt you. I like to think of them as smoke and mirrors because they are really just illusions.

My experience with addiction led me to where I saw it was just an illusion. That no substance actually had any power over me. Once I saw this completely for each of my addictions, the battle was over and I have not returned to them.

I lived in fear my whole life until I had processed enough of the trauma and come to terms with what had happened to me. The flashbacks and fear almost completely vanished and it no longer dominates my life.

That last example reveals an important point. A lot of our paradigm shifts are the updating of beliefs that were formed when we were very young and still developing, which continues until we are about 25 years old. And many of them are preverbal, meaning that we hold them as strong views but do not have the words to express them since they formed in us before our speech developed.

There is no shame in these beliefs because you didn't choose to form them. You didn't know any better than what was presented to you at the time. But, now, a lot of them stand in the way of the life you're aiming for.

Allow your long-held beliefs to be shifted to give yourself the best chance of reaching your goals.

All You Have is Now

Most of us fixate on either the past or the future rather than being fully present in the *now* moment. Some physicists believe that time is an illusion and all we actually have is now. But, regardless of your standpoint, the reality is that the only moment we have to make a difference to our lives is now. If you want to make changes, it's now. If you want to quit an addiction, now is the only time you can do it. But if you're not ready yet, that's fine. That just means *now* is the time for something else. Maybe rest or preparation.

Living in the *now* doesn't mean you can't make plans. Plans are what we're talking about in this book. But, even when you think about the future, there is a difference between whether you're thinking about it from the present moment or getting lost in the fantasy of it as though you were already there. I'm not suggesting that's always bad. But as I've already shared, I lived in my own future fantasy for a long time. I was putting all my energy into creating a life in a world and time that didn't yet exist and dissociating from the past that was so full of pain and regret. The consequence was never being present in the *now* moments, so never really engaging with life and achieving very little.

Living in the now also doesn't mean you can't revisit the past. In fact, I hope to show in this book that there is no avoiding doing that. Those of us that want to avoid the past do so because of trauma and regrets and because we don't believe there is any way to redeem what has already taken place. So, we are bound to revisit it endlessly.

My future-fantasy years were a response to the many years I'd spent previously going over and over the same painful events in my mind – things that had happened to me, stupid things I'd said, moments where I'd missed an opportunity and couldn't get it back. It was torture.

I completely understand the pull of the past and the future. But, if you want to build a solid life that lasts, it needs to ground you firmly in the *now*. Life is now.

Put aside your regrets, lay down your plans, and be with yourself for a while.

Nothing is as it Seems

Most religions draw a line between the spiritual and physical realms. And today, we talk about something being 'real', meaning that it is physical as in solid. This has largely come from the influences of religion on science and vice versa.

However, as quantum physics reveals more and more about the reality of the world, we can see that the so-called physical world is nothing of the sort. A 'solid' object, like a chair or table, has more space between the particles of matter than the actual matter itself.

A few years ago, many believed that we inherited our genes from our parents and there was little we could do about it. It is now possible for scientists to observe changes on a genetic level referred to as gene expression. This understanding does away with the idea of us all being hard-wired a certain way and unable to fundamentally change, replacing it with the concept of being able to change on even the deepest level of our DNA.

There is a depth to this universe and to us that we will never fully fathom. I hope this book will help open up the infinite possibilities that exist so you can begin to expect that things will actually happen outside of your ability to conceive of them right now. That means letting go of some of the control and allowing the process to take place *in* you.

Nothing is as it seems. And that's good because it means that there's always the possibility that it's better than it's seemed so far.

Meeting Yourself for the First Time

"You... meet you."

We rely completely on other people for the first few years of our lives, and then when we're old enough to stand on our own two feet, society expects that we will fit in for the rest of our years. This can leave us without a sense of ourselves and who we really are.

This process will lead you to a point where you meet yourself for the first time. If it hasn't already happened for you, it will. For me, this is one of the most memorable experiences because it was so profound. I realised in that moment that I had lived my whole life vicariously. I interpreted my every thought and action through the lens of what other people would think, feel, and do. And had no idea whatsoever who I was or what I wanted.

In that moment, I glimpsed who I was for the first time and realised that I was a person in my own right.

In order to have the life you're longing for, you need to be comfortable with yourself and who you really are.

We did the groundwork for this in *Your Structural Survey,* so I hope this concept is feeling more comfortable.

Meeting yourself can be one of the most liberating experiences you'll ever have.

It's All On You

This next one is a biggie. For me, it was both scary and liberating.

You hold the ultimate power of choice in your life. Nothing and no one can ever take that away from you. And nobody can *make* you do anything.

I know that reading that last sentence might make you squirm, and there may be some objections coming up in your mind right now. I understand. But it really is true. It doesn't mean nothing will ever happen to you that you don't like. It doesn't mean that no one can ever do anything to you without your permission. But what it means is that you ultimately have the power of choice in your life. You get to choose your response to what happens to you.

This paradigm shift came during some of the darkest years of my life. I felt completely powerless to change anything. I would decide I was going to stop drinking, and then a few hours later, my legs would take me there and I didn't know how to stop it from happening. One time when I was a teenager, my family had me under something like 'house arrest' and were all downstairs in the living room. I knew I couldn't get past the living room and out the front door without them noticing, and the urge was so great to drink that I jumped out of the first-floor window. I snuck through the garden and made it to the local nightclub in time to buy a round of drinks and down them before closing time.

Years later, once I had started to see that I had the power to choose, I gave everything in me to stop drinking. I would go to the shop to get some alcohol, buy a four-pack, take a sip, then tip the rest away. I would be back later to buy some more. Sometimes I would walk a few steps down the road, but wanting to fight it, I'd turn around and walk a few steps back. Then the urge would get the better of me, so I'd turn around again and walk a few steps the other way, and so on for hours.

If you are as stuck as I was, don't despair. You have the power to make any changes you desire in your life. Not right this second. But in the end. Stopping drinking took me decades, as did other things like finding a place to call my home. And, as I'll keep saying, it was worth every second.

So, it's all on you. And that's good news. Because that is your superpower.

Ultimately, you get to choose it all.

You *Were* a Victim

If someone abused you or took advantage of you at any point in the past, you were a victim. There is no exception to that. If you were a child, you can never be to blame for what happened to you. And, if you were an adult, you were not to blame either, even when issues like consent confuse the matter, making it seem less clear. It is sometimes necessary and helpful to identify our involvement so that we can take responsibility for our part and do our best to ensure that the same thing doesn't happen again. But you have to be careful with this because being a victim can so easily lead to feeling like you *are* to blame. You might need help to navigate this.

Throughout my life, I have been the victim of abuses that fit into all those scenarios. I have learnt to refuse the blame that comes with the abuses that happened when I was a child, absolving myself of responsibility. There are some abusive incidents that happened when I was an adult that I see in the same way because I didn't play any part in them. Then there were other incidents where I could see that I *did* play a part in what took place. It was not comfortable, but I knew I needed to face up to that and take responsibility for my part in what happened. Not to the other person, but just with myself.

Recently, Clare and I were watching *Celebrity SAS: Who Dares Wins*, a series that puts celebrities through a gruelling selection process similar to SAS selection. Ex-special forces instructors, called DS (Directing Staff), help to run the program led by the chief instructor.

Every episode, the DS pulls at least one person into a room to grill them and see if they can get under their skin. In this particular episode, former Premier League footballer, Kieron Dyer, was pulled in because two of the DS wanted to discuss an earlier exercise – a "kill or be killed" scenario – where the participants had to take it in turns to attack one of the DS and not stop until they were told to. When it was his turn, Dyer had tackled the DS to the floor and laid into him relentlessly, shouting "F*** you! F*** you!" The DS wanted to find out what was behind that aggression.

Dyer opened up and shared about being sexually abused when he was younger, describing the lasting effects it had had on him.

After sharing that it had turned him into a monster and how he'd hurt so many people as a result, including his family, he said, "And I always have the mindset of 'do you know what? Because I'm a victim, this is the way I am'." He continued, "From today, when I come out of here, I am not a victim of sexual abuse. No more. Because every time I'm a victim, he wins. Every time I hurt my family, he wins."

It was obvious his experience moved the instructors, and Clare and I felt moved too.

After Dyer left the room, the DS turned to the senior instructor and said, "He was a victim." The senior instructor said, "He was. He's not anymore." And the DS echoed with, "The word's *'was'*."[18]

---

[18] "Adversity." Celebrity SAS: Who Dares Wins, Minnow Films 2019. Channel 4, https://www.channel4.com/programmes/celebrity-sas-who-dares-wins/on-demand/71228-004

That's powerful! The heart of it all is what is behind the 'Me too' movement – I'm no longer a victim, I'm a survivor.

In Darrell Hammond's exceptional documentary, *Cracked Up*, about his life, he starts to talk about mental illness and then corrects himself saying, "Let's call it what it is – mental injury."[19] That resonates with me so deeply because I can now see that all the madness and torment I experienced for so many years resulted from the things that were done to me by others. I blamed and punished myself for so long, but none of it was my fault. On top of that, people shamed me for years about my drinking and other behaviour when I didn't know how to stop, or even why I was doing it. That behaviour was not my choice. It resulted from the choices other people – adults – made towards me when I was helpless to do anything about it.

It is completely understandable if you still see yourself as a victim and there is no shame in it. But, you don't have to stay there. This is one of the greatest uses of your superpower we were just talking about. You didn't choose what happened to you and you *were* a victim, but you get to choose whether that's where you stay. The good side of this is that you get to take back control, which is something that gets obliterated when you are a victim.

The distinction I find helpful is that while what happened to me was not and is still not my fault, my life is my responsibility now as an adult. So, if anything's ever going to change, it's going to change because I take charge of myself and my life to change it proactively.

I know this may not be easy to hear, but I am saying it out of love and compassion because the results of this is what I'm living right now. Being the victim of other people's actions dictated my entire experience of life. I didn't choose what they did to me. But, if I stayed there, I couldn't also have my dream life. For me, when it comes down to a choice between staying the victim or having my dream life, the choice is clear. I can't live

---

[19] *Cracked Up: The Darrell Hammond Story*. Directed by Michelle Esrick, Ripple Effect films, 2018. Netflix, https://www.netflix.com/title/81162153

on this earth without moving away from the agony of the past, towards an actual life full of good things. I can't see any point in that.

My whole life, people made me feel like everything was my fault. In my family, it was a shared joke. "Blame it on Adrian, ha, ha!" My siblings were innocent in this. They were victims of a lot of the same things I was. They didn't realise the effect it was having on my worldview. I still face the feeling that everything is my fault daily, and it is so convincing. I think of the trauma and all its effects as something I'm *doing* rather than something that's *happening* to me because of other people's choices.

I waited so long for someone to come along and rescue me, not realising that they weren't ever going to come, and I didn't need them to, in order to get free.

If you feel you can't accept what I'm saying here, I fully get it. I don't want to pressure you and I don't want to make things harder for you. I just want to be the person who tells you the truth because I can't bear the idea of you never getting to hear it.

You do what's best for you.

Remove All Unnecessary Pressure

This one will get other people's backs up. We live in a world where 'busy' is cool and you're expected to pull your weight and be part of society and fit in with the crowd. Many people don't like it if you opt out of these things. But those people aren't living your life.

If you're serious about your life, this is something that you need to pay attention to. You can't keep living the way you have and expect different results. And there's a lot of excess that has nothing to do with what you're building. This just adds unnecessary pressure to your life.

I warn you that this will be disruptive. It is actually offensive to people if you dare to not be busy and choose not to take part in the things that they do.

Unnecessary pressure comes from too much, from the wrong type of things, from trying to have more than one priority, and from trying to please others. These all hinder rather than help the process of self-development.

In 2014, I decided I was going to go off to the Yukon on my own for six months. I contacted everyone I knew and told them what I was doing and asked them to give me space. This wasn't for fun. I was doing it to save my life because I knew things had to change drastically. However, it didn't take long to realise that it was going to cost a lot of money, and since I didn't have any, I didn't get any further than my bedroom door. But nobody knew this. So, for a long time after, people left me in peace and I got to focus on myself and just work on my heart.

Now, I know that when I talk about removing all unnecessary pressure, you're thinking, 'But what about work, and the kids, and church, and the charity work I volunteer for?' Only you can say which of those things is necessary. For me, it was literally a matter of life and death, so I was willing to do whatever.

If your life is stable and you can honestly say you're not heading for an imminent crisis, then removing all unnecessary pressure may mean doing nothing quite that drastic. But that doesn't mean you won't have to make some hard decisions. A lot of the things we do that involve other people are simply not essential. And when it comes down to a choice between what really matters and what doesn't, sometimes we matter more. We will look at this more later in *Going Against the Tribe*.

Only you can decide what really matters in your life and determine what is actually just unnecessary pressure. But if this process is your priority, there will be things that will definitely need to go.

Fork in the Road Moments

Most paradigm shift moments involve some level of decision from you. They almost never happen completely randomly and outside of your control. They come because of your diligent pursuit of new understanding.

There is a kind of paradigm shift I call a fork in the road moment. It is the moment where your life hangs in the balance, waiting for you to decide which way to go. The choice is not clear and often you only find out later that the way that looked most appealing would have been disastrous, and the way that looked like the path to hell was actually the path to life.

In my mind, the left fork (probably because I'm right-handed) is the one that looks like it would be the easiest to take. You can see that it carries on naturally in the way that you've been heading up to that point. It is wide and straight. The right fork hardly looks like a path at all, and giant obstacles block the way.

The picture develops to show that the left-hand fork actually loops back quickly to where the fork began, or even beyond it, but now you're heading in the opposite direction. The right-hand fork quickly opens up and reveals itself as the best way to get ahead.

My most recent fork-in-the-road moment was deciding whether to go ahead with this book. Choosing the left-hand fork would have been to carry on thinking about writing a book *someday* and continuing to learn about new ways to do it. That way appeared clear, with little risk. But, soon enough, I would probably have given up on my dream and ended up somewhere I didn't want to be. The right-hand fork involved massive commitment and me putting myself out there when I prefer anonymity and privacy.

Writing the first draft has proven to me that I made the right choice. I can see that this way leads forward because of the changes I've experienced in myself and the joy I have from sharing my ideas with other people.

When Clare and I faced the decision, it was 100% NOT clear which fork was the best to take. We had to come back to our *1/5/10 Plan*, get in touch with our values, and decide if we could handle another risk, on the back of many others, before we had any idea which way to go. From this side, it looks so obvious. But beforehand, it was not at all clear until the point where we had committed.

A great parallel is Neo's red pill/blue pill moment[20] in *The Matrix*. He had to make the choice of which to take. The left fork is the blue pill. If you take that pill, you can forget that you ever had any dreams for your life and carry on oblivious. The red pill is the right-hand fork. It means you are going to have to see life as it really is, but at least then you're actually dealing with reality, not an illusion.

So, when you come to a fork in the road, get out *Your 1/5/10 Plan* and ask, "Which fork leads to my goals?" If you're going to stay true to yourself and your plan, there isn't much thinking to do. I've always found that as soon as I make the choice, all the fears, doubts, uncertainties and every other obstacle I face just melts away. That doesn't mean you won't face them again. Sorry! But, you will have broken the back of them.

---

[20] *The Matrix*. Directed by Lana Wachowski & Lilly Wachowski, theatrical version. Los Angeles, California: Silver Pictures, Warner Bros, Village Roadshow Pictures. 1999.

15

WHEN LIFE WON'T LET UP
Always Be Prepared

It all feels too much.

One thing follows another and now you're in a state of panic.

You're caught in a hurricane and you can't see how to escape.

You just want to curl up in a ball and shut it all out.

But you know there are consequences if you do.

And the last time you did, everything fell apart – friendships, work, your mental health, and making progress towards your dreams.

So, what should you do?

If You Batten Down the Hatches, You May Perish

There's a storm coming. You don't know when and you don't know how bad, but one thing's for sure, it's coming. It might be redundancy, or a scary diagnosis, the death of a loved one, or robbery. It might be completely internal because of your fragile state – you wake up one day and simply can't go on. You've had enough.

It is foolish to go through life ignoring that these events are bound to happen. They won't all happen, but one or more of them happening in your lifetime is a guarantee.

Like the Scout Motto instructs, it's best to "Be prepared". Always.

The Scout's founder, Baden-Powell, wrote that 'Be Prepared,' means "you are always in a state of readiness in mind and body to do your duty."[21]

Sometimes the best course of action is to board up the house and steel yourself against the wind. But there are also times when this will not save you. No matter how desperate you are to hide inside and try to ignore the howling gale, you need to dig deep and tap into your last reserves to survive.

In those moments, it can appear you have absolutely nothing left to give. But in my experience, this is never true.

2019 brought my last major crisis, when the new memories of abuse as a child finally surfaced. After so many years of pushing on and facing whatever came up, this was the point where I wanted to give up like never before.

By that point, flashbacks bombarded me day and night and I had become physically dependent on alcohol again. It was a total nightmare. At points, I couldn't hold the alcohol down because my body was rejecting it and I had to go to hospital. The nurse told me I had to keep on drinking. I faced wave after wave of unbearable feelings and the constant temptation to kill myself to get relief.

The less drastic solution would have been to get into bed, pull the covers over my head, and just stay there. And, for the first time, I knew I could actually do it and no one would judge me because they would now know what had happened to me. I had a reason for how much I struggled. Clare and I were living with her parents, and *I* had a stability that I'd never experienced. I didn't have any of the negative motivations that had pressured me to keep going in the past, when I was facing everything

---

[21] Brian Wendell. "Be Prepared: The Origin Story behind the Scout Motto." Bryan on Scouting, Boy Scouts of America, 2017, blog.scoutingmagazine.org/2017/05/08/be-prepared-scout-motto-origin.

alone. I had a roof over my head, I wouldn't go hungry, and Clare's parents would not kick us out.

But I could see that I was at a fork in the road and if I went to my bed, there was no guarantee of survival. As I remembered my dreams, which appeared more impossible than ever, I knew I had to find that true grit within and push on once again.

All I could do was my best to stay in the moment, hold on to my dreams, and face each internal assault as it happened.

During this time, Clare and I paid for me to see a psychologist for trauma treatment. She sent out three self-assessments for me to do before our first meeting. The first two were to measure your depression and anxiety levels over the last few weeks. My score was the highest possible – meaning I was extremely depressed and anxious. And the third was for trauma in which I scored all questions the highest possible, apart from two which I didn't feel were relevant. This showed I was extremely traumatised. When I got to the appointment, the psychologist couldn't believe that I had actually turned up. When she reviewed the tests, she was certain that I'd be a no-show, and planned something else to do during my slot.

Why did I go to that appointment when I was feeling as bad as I was? Because I knew I had to find a way through what I was facing. It was a matter of life or death. If I didn't eventually succumb to suicide, the alcohol would eventually get the better of me. Plus, the effect on Clare was unbearable to see. I had nothing in me to do anything and this came after 20 years of giving it all without the results I wanted to see. But there were things that were more important to me than all of that. Achieving my dreams. And the woman I love with all my heart.

If I had battened down the hatches, it would have been the death of me, I'm sure. Instead, I pushed on one more time, not knowing whether there was really any point. But this time, it was the last time in relation to so much of what I had faced for 30 years and I finally got my relief.

There will be stormy days in your life at some point. That's not a prophecy of doom. It's a warning to prepare. And, when you feel like jacking it all in, just hold on a bit longer because you never know when you're going to get your victory.

I promise it will come.

Become Comfortable Being Uncomfortable

As you already know, this life is seriously hard work. Advertising and media sell a dream where you lounge around all day and never have to lift a finger. But in reality, every single day you need to graft to stay alive, to survive, and even more so, if you want to thrive. Yes, you can engineer things so you don't have to graft until your dying breath. But you can't start off there. For now, you need to be prepared to give whatever it takes to overcome whatever you face.

Hard, but true.

For me, this was an unbearable realisation because, when I saw it, there was literally nothing about my life that I liked or wanted. Mental illness, addiction, relative poverty, pain, exhaustion, inability to produce results, nobody I felt I could trust. And the list goes on.

After years of not trusting anybody, I dared to contact a therapist to get help again with my struggles. In our sessions, she would often say to me that my healing and recovery was going to take years or decades because of how severely out of balance I was. Sometimes I nodded and smiled. Other times, I contested the point. And, always, I smugly thought to myself, "What does she know? I'm different from everyone else and I know I can get through this quicker than them."

But she was right. There was no way to get from where I was to a place of freedom without years of hard slog. So, what's the point if it's going to be that hard? I'll repeat this many times because it's so important – it's worth whatever effort it takes to achieve your wildest dreams. And when that day finally comes, when you stand back and look at what you've built, the years of pain and heartache will melt away.

In the movie, *Click*, Adam Sandler's character receives a magic remote control which enables him to alter reality. After realising he can skip the parts that he'd rather not go through, he quickly becomes unable to stop and skips years of his life. For a long time, that's what I was like. I was constantly rushing to try to speed up the time I knew it would take to overcome everything I faced. I wanted what was on the other side of the process, but I didn't want to have to go *through* the process to get there. In *Click*, he ends up fast-forwarding through his entire life, missing out on all the best bits as well.[22]

The irony is that the more we try to rush and force the process of change, the more we interfere with its progress and actually prolong it.

One indicator of how comfortable you are with being *uncomfortable* is your ability to sit still in silence. We looked at this earlier in the section containing *Your Structural Survey*. Our modern world has endless potential distractions, and it is much easier to go from one distraction to the next than get in touch with what's going on inside.

Here's an example of what I'm talking about:

Years ago, I went to my friend Bob's flat and let myself in. When I got there, he was sitting in a chair. Nothing strange about that, you say. But there *was* something strange about it. He didn't have a phone in his hand, or the TV on. He was just sitting extremely still, deep in thought. It actually freaked me out because it wasn't (and still isn't) something you see people doing.

Bob is one of the deepest and most insightful people I know. He has also changed more than nearly anyone I know. He is unrecognisable from the person I met 30 years ago. There's a connection between that story

---

[22] *Click*. Directed by Frank Coraci, theatrical version. Los Angeles, California: Columbian Pictures Revolution Studios, Happy Madison Productions. 2006.

and Bob's transformation. He learnt to become comfortable being uncomfortable, and it eventually led to lasting change.

Blaise Pascal, a 17th-century scientist and philosopher, agrees:

"All of humanity's problems stem from man's inability to sit quietly in a room alone."[23]

My years spent mostly in bed because of chronic pain and fatigue taught me how to be alone with myself without distraction. There were times I felt so unbearable, I didn't know how to make it through the next second. For a long time, I would watch endless TV on my laptop or read when I had it in me to numb out and not have to look at everything I faced. But in those times where it was just me and the silence, I began to learn contentment despite my circumstances. A painful but necessary lesson.

If you can learn to sit in a chair with no distractions and feel at peace or even happy, then you have achieved something amazing. It means you don't need to add to or change anything about your life to be content in that moment. You don't need to seek answers outside yourself. You don't constantly need to chase something *out there*.

Just to *be* is powerful.

So, I urge you to become comfortable being uncomfortable so you can take everything that life is going to throw at you in your stride.

Face Up to What's Inside

The hardest thing you'll ever do is face what's inside yourself and learn to let go of what you've been clinging to. We all seem to shy away from it, and as the world modernises, we move further away from the skills required to deal with the deeper self. The more you suffered as a child, the harder it is to look inside, and if you don't have people around you that support that way of thinking, it only makes it harder again.

---

[23] Pascal, Blaise, and G. Ruffini. *Pensées*. 1st ed. Gianluca, 2017.Kindle.

I searched for years for any other way than to have to face what was inside me. I tried to imagine a different world where I could just ignore the chasm inside and get on with the life I wanted now. But, even though I would feel good for a time, it would never last, and would always lead back to facing the pain anyway.

The irony is, when we don't face the pain of a trauma early on, it has the potential to doom us to facing it moment by moment for the rest of our lives. And we may be so shut off from what happened, we don't recognise that it is the cause. But it is a thread of unresolved trauma and pain that runs through our lives. Much like dry rot that gradually eats away at the house from the inside. The paintwork may be intact, but underneath, the wood is slowly crumbling to pieces.

In order to cope, we may compartmentalise the trauma by splitting off from the part that was affected. We build a life but can never fully engage with it or enjoy it in all its fullness. But we can never fully escape its effects and few of us make it to our death bed without having to look at what's really inside. But let's say you manage this gargantuan feat. Is it really something you'll be proud of? It feels so important now to protect what you've built so far, maintain the status quo, keep everyone else happy, and not complain. But, in those last moments, when you look back, what will you really feel? Compare that to looking back on a life where you gave and faced everything?

Many studies have proven that in those final moments, people are unavoidably faced with themselves and the success (or failure) of their life. Those studies show people regret not spending time with their family, and not taking more risks. Not going for the dream job when they had the chance. No one regrets not spending more time at the office or making more money. But there is also no mention of "I wish I'd held it all together more or impressed more people with my stoicism".

When, at 18, I decided I needed to turn my life around because I was so out of control, I didn't realise what I was letting myself in for. And like

Neo's red pill/blue pill moment,[24] I could never unsee what a mess my life had become. I could never put the lid back on and go back to being ignorant of where all my struggles were coming from – not outside me, but deep inside me.

The best example from my life of burying pain deep and refusing to look at it was over the death of my dad when I was eight years old. I carried the pain and confusion around for over a decade before I felt able to grieve and cry over losing him. My reasons were very complex and confused. They were the reasoning of an eight-year-old. But, in that moment during a counselling session when the floodgates opened, I had my first experience of wondering, "Why the hell have I been so afraid of this?" It felt amazing. All that agony flowing out of me instead of bouncing around inside me day after day, being triggered by every emotion.

Facing yourself and all your pain and grief is the hardest thing you'll ever do. But if you don't do it proactively and make it a habit, you will do it many times more throughout your life. You just may not realise that's what's happening. It's important to say again at this point that I'm not talking about digging for the sake of it. I'm saying that if there are things you've been avoiding and hiding from, you can begin to notice and inquire about them. And, as always, if it's not safe to do it on your own, find someone to help you. Preferably a professional.

Going Against the Tribe: The Second Hardest Thing You'll Ever Do

Once you decide you are going to change your life for the better, you are guaranteed to experience a backlash from people around you – your tribe.

The tribe is not your enemy. Just the opposite is true. They are your family, allies, and closest friends. That's what makes it so hard to go against them and so surprising when they can seem to be so against you.

---

[24] *The Matrix*. Directed by Lana Wachowski & Lilly Wachowski, theatrical version. Los Angeles, California: Silver Pictures, Warner Bros, Village Roadshow Pictures. 1999.

Rudyard Kipling said it like this:

"The individual has always had to struggle to keep from being overwhelmed by the tribe. To be your own man is a hard business. If you try it, you'll be lonely often, and sometimes frightened. But no price is too high to pay for the privilege of owning yourself."[25]

Even though the tribe is not your enemy, they can come across that way in response to you building your life. When you choose a way that is not the way of your culture, whether that's the culture of your country, your people group, your religion, your group of friends, or whoever, it can cause a violent reaction. People can't easily stay neutral in their response because, when *you* choose a different way, you are calling into question the way they do things or the way they've always been done.

When the tribe seems to be against you, it is not really you they are against, but the principles that you are standing for. When you are first starting out, the new ways you are trying to establish are like the fragile sapling that we talked about earlier. A funny look from someone you respect or care about can be enough to throw you off your game.

If you hold your ground and do your best to ride it out, there will come a time when it no longer bothers you. The irony is that once you reach this point, people will also be more receptive to what you have to say because you have already established yourself in it, so it comes with proof. That's the thing. Most people need to see proof before they'll believe anything at all. And, at first, all the evidence of change is deep inside you, so there is nothing on the surface for others to look at.

I imagine it like this: when we first decide we are moving away from a concept or idea and towards something else, it creates a vacuum. Or, there was really only a vacuum there in the first place because we'd never formed our own views and opinions. When we bump into other

---

[25] Gordon, Arthur, and Rudyard Kipling. "Six Hours with Rudyard Kipling." Kipling, vol. 2, 1983, pp. 383–87. Crossref, doi:10.1007/978-1-349-05109-0_49.

people, the force of their conviction about what they believe is greater than the vacuum of our new idea and uncertainty. Without even meaning to, the other person fills us up with their idea and we don't know what to believe anymore.

As we allow our own conviction and assurance to build on the inside of us, until the pressure on the inside is equal or greater than the pressure in others, they are no longer a threat to us and we can share what we believe without the resistance from other people, so neither side adopts a defensive position.

If your life is a mess and nothing seems to work for you, it is very hard to go against the tribe because you appear to be in a weaker position. I experienced this precarious position most when I saw a way forward with addiction that was unorthodox or against what those around me thought was best. People were convinced they knew better, and I could understand why. But, if I hadn't been able to make my own choices from that position, I would still be there and never have grown up or got free.

I am not exaggerating when I say that when I went against my tribe, I felt like I might die. The feelings were so intense that I actually thought it would kill me. The fear of being ostracised and lonely is a kind of living death, or even worse than dying, so this feeling really makes sense.

Now, I have healthy, growing relationships with the people that seemed to be so against me. And I have come to see that they were never really against me at all.

Often, when people attack your ideas about change, they are just speaking to you from their own fear. They are sitting in a cave, saying, "Don't go outside, it's dangerous." When you ask, "What's outside the cave?" They can't actually tell you. So, you ask, "Have you ever actually been outside the cave?" They haven't, but they've been told their whole lives that it's dangerous out there. Often, people are actually trying to protect you. They don't realise they're actually holding you back.

Going against the tribe is the second hardest thing, partly *because* facing what's inside yourself is the hardest thing. What I mean by that is, you're not simply saying, 'I think I'm going to paint my lounge green' to someone who doesn't really like green. You are saying to them by your words and actions that you are going to face what's inside you – and this scares people silly because they are not ready to do it themselves. They know that if they do that, they will have to go against their tribe, and it could mean rejection or ostracism.

Going against the tribe is not a position of superiority. It's about stages of development. When I was part of the tribe in a religious environment, I would debate and argue with anyone who opposed or threatened my point of view because I was afraid of what it would mean if I didn't have something certain to cling to. Indoctrination conditioned me to believe that free thought was dangerous and would elicit disapproval. We all do this to each other at some point in our lives. It's good to remember this when someone is doing it to you.

One of the greatest obstacles you'll face when choosing to go against the tribe is believing it is impossible to give up your current contribution to the world and all the things you've committed to. In reality, no one will miss you too much and the world may just be better off without your mess while you get yourself sorted out.

We can see the power of the tribe most powerfully across borders where the culture is completely different. A border is just a few metres across. The people on either side of the border are not that different. They often share the same ancestors. So, why the wildly different culture? My simple answer to this is the tribe. It's group-think. It's the powerful effect we have on each other when we come together, where individuals or factions with powerful ideas influence the many and it either works for or against the whole.

All it takes is one person to go against the tribe, to turn the world upside down. For good or for evil. A Hitler against the sanctity of all life. Or a Rosa Parks against collective racism, for example.

Going against the tribe is the hardest thing you'll have to do in this process after facing up to what's inside you. But once you establish yourself for who you truly are, you will find that you build up a new tribe of like-minded people around you, including some of the same people that seemed to be against you. And, as you go through your transformation, you will draw other people to yourself who are in the same process as you. If you know nobody like that right now, remember I'm cheering you on.

We are all conditioned to care deeply about what others think about us. And when that 'others' means everyone around us, it makes it many times harder. But when you approach the end, are you going to look back and think 'I'm so glad I pleased everyone else'? Or, 'I'm so glad I was true to myself'?

I know which I prefer.

Autonomy

Autonomy means that you are in a self-governing state. You have taken control of yourself, your life, and the direction you're heading in.

Studies show that autonomy makes people healthier, gives them a longer life, and keeps them alert and happy.

Social psychologist and researcher, Angus Campbell, agrees:

"Having a strong sense of controlling one's life is a more dependable predictor of positive feelings of well-being than any of the objective conditions of life we have considered."[26]

---

[26] Salmansohn, Karen. "The No. 1 Contributor to Happiness." Psychology Today, Sussex Publishers, LLC, 2011, www.psychologytoday.com/gb/blog/bouncing-back/201106/the-no-1-contributor-happiness#:%7E:text=Researcher%20Angus%20Campbell%20emphatically%20endorses,have%20considered%2C%22%20says%20Campbell.

My desire for autonomy was one of the specific things that people opposed in the early days of my process. I so heavily depended on other people and what they thought of me, I didn't really have a life of my own. I knew that breaking away from people was necessary to discover my identity before coming back to them again. But others couldn't see this because I appeared so incapable and my decisions so easily led to disaster. So, they fought my attempts at autonomy.

It is within each of us to make something of ourselves. If you want to lead a truly fulfilling life, you need to take charge because you're the only one who can.

Be courageous and trust that inner voice that's guiding you to better things.

Expect the Unexpected

This is one of my favourite oxymorons and it actually makes sense. What it means is that as long as you are aware that things can come out of nowhere at any moment, you can be prepared to handle them when they do.

My favourite thriller novel protagonist, Jack Reacher, says it like this:

"Hope for the best, plan for the worst."[27]

And:

"Plans go to hell as soon as the first shot is fired."[28]

Just like going into battle, when we enter this process, we are treading into unknown territory and, of course, we hope the process will go smoothly and without a hitch. But we are also wise to put things in place

---

[27] Child, Lee. 2015. "Persona." Jack Reacher 19 (B). 1st ed., London, GB: Bantam Books.
[28] Child, Lee. 2010. "61 Hours." Jack Reacher 14. 1st ed., London, GB: Bantam Books.

to take care of everything we can't see in advance but know is likely to happen.

One way that I did this during my years of sickness in bed was preparing for the time after I got better by learning as much as I could. I had an expectation, despite appearances, that my sickness would not last forever. All that learning encouraged me about the possibilities available to turn my life around. And it helped me to understand all the mistakes other people had made so that I didn't have to go through unnecessary struggles. As they say, a wise man learns from the errors of others. Instead of starting from scratch once I had recovered enough, I was raring to go with everything that I'd prepared during my years in bed.

Another wise saying is:

"Insure what you can't afford to lose."

Clare and I have contents and accidental damage insurance on the flat we rent. We've never needed it yet and are unlikely to, but we are not in a position to cover the cost of the damage if the flat burns down or we get robbed.

Likewise, after I went through my last crisis, my care coordinator from the recovery team helped me to put together a crisis plan to mitigate against any unnecessary damage if a crisis hits. Back then, I was continually on the edge of crisis and the plan was always at the back of my mind. The stronger and the more stable I've become, the less I need that crisis plan. I rarely think about it anymore, just like I don't think about the contents and accidental damage insurance. But if a crisis hits, I'm covered and know exactly what I need to do.

Leave nothing to chance when it comes to what matters most to you. Hope for the best, but also plan for the worst. Because the worst might just happen.

And if it does, you'll be glad you were prepared.

16

TAKING CHARGE LIKE A BOSS
The Buck Stops with You

You started with a bang.

You feel like you're actually getting somewhere now.

Making good progress towards your goals.

You're clear on what's required and you've even survived your first battle with one of your tribe.

Undeterred, you push on.

But then you realise you're way out of your comfort zone, where you've lived for as long as you can remember.

It was safe. You always knew where you were with everything and rarely felt challenged. Now life is a continual learning process. And you face more and more decisions every day.

It feels scary and you're worried you've made a mistake.

You wonder how hard it would be to get your old life back.

What's it all for, anyway?

Life Design, Your Way

There is no greater privilege than being able to craft and sculpt a life just for you. On a surface level, our lives look pretty similar. We all need the same things to survive and we all must work every day to ensure we have them. But, once you take care of these basic needs, there is a beautiful world to explore full of amazing people to get to know.

The more you can see beyond the mundanity of your existence, the more you'll have moments of pure joy, as you imagine everything you could do with your life. And, it's not just the big stuff that you wrote in *Your 1/5/10 Plan*, it's the details as well. Like finding a cafe near your home that does a Swiss water organic decaf coffee that tastes amazing and doesn't make you feel too wired or tired (that's one of my joys, in case you wondered). Or, realising that you love walking and talking about life in the open country with your friends, so you book in times to make that happen (also one of mine).

Depending on your viewpoint, we are all the same or we are all completely unique. Maybe Swiss water decaf sounds boring as hell to you. As well as walking and talking with your friends for fun. And that's fine. I'm me, and you're you. But what I'm trying to convey is the joy of discovering who you really are on the inside and designing every aspect of your life to match that.

I can't think of a greater privilege in this world than designing my own life the way I choose.

Can you?

Who You Are is not Yet Decided

We come into this world innocent and impressionable. We're a blank canvas. There are attributes we inherit from our parents, but so much is yet to be decided.

And the same is still true today. Nothing about you is set in stone. There have been some good things and some hard things that formed your view of yourself, and it is all subject to change.

This is a subset of life design, in that you have control over who you are and who you want to become. It's not set in stone.

After my dad died, my mum had a lovely home-help who came around once a week to do things like ironing and cleaning, as my mum was recovering from major surgery. One day, the home-help looked at me and said, "You'll either be a millionaire or you'll end up in prison. And I'll be able to tell people, 'I knew him when he was little, and ironed his boxer shorts'." I'm sure this was in response to the extreme nature of my behaviour.

That observation was a fork-in-the-road observation of sorts. She could see that I was going to do something big, and I had the potential for something great or really destructive. A few times I spent a night in a cell, but somehow avoided prison by some miracle. I am not a millionaire yet, but I am working my way there.

There was a lot of insight in what that lovely home-help saw.

When I was at rehab for drugs and alcohol, one of the senior staff called me into his office to talk about why I had relapsed in the last phase of the program. I saw it as an opportunity to open up and bare my heart because it seemed like he genuinely wanted to know why it had happened.

I spent the next few vulnerable minutes talking about the things that had led to my substance abuse, like my dad dying and depression. When I finished, he said, "I'll tell you what your problem is." I sat forward in my seat in anticipation of the answer he was going to give about all my problems. "You're lazy and have an excuse for everything," he said. His words left me stunned, and I immediately shut down.

It was a long time before I opened up to anyone again.

That man couldn't have been more wrong about me. But, those words still cause me to doubt myself today because he was so convinced and so convincing. I've had to fight those words and many more misjudgements about my character my whole life. And instead, hold on to the fact that who I am is not yet fully decided. It may be many years before I, or anyone else, see who I really am because only history tells the whole truth.

Over the years, a few people tried to force me to accept the label of alcoholic and, as I've said before, I refused. I refused because their definition was hopeless. Their definition meant I would always remain that way as it was a part of my identity. The only hope they were offering was a lifetime of abstinence, but no resolution to the agony underneath. What some have called a dry drunk. I jumped through those hoops many times but never got free on the inside. I could not agree with them and damn myself to a life of imprisonment just to please them. Even though I had struggled with alcohol for decades, I would not agree that this was all I'd ever be.

Don't be quick to pigeonhole yourself or let anyone else do it to you. Who you are is up for grabs and is waiting to be discovered on the inside of you.

One of the best things you can do with your decision-making abilities is to not leave your identity and character to chance. Be proactive about forming and shaping who you are. Only you can ultimately decide what that is.

Let Peace Be Your Guide

The more you connect with who you really are, the more at ease you become with yourself and the more you can trust yourself. As a result, you can learn to get in touch with what many of us call our gut – our instinct – and learn to trust that too.

Over the years, I have learnt to trust my gut for all major life decisions. This is especially true when I'm at one of those fork-in-the-road moments. The deciding factor is often just that one fork presents itself as having more of a sense of peace than the other. The other fork has more of a sense of conflict and uneasiness. This does not mean that I feel completely peaceful. Often, it's just the opposite. It's that in the middle of all the churning that's going on around a decision, when I focus on the one option versus the other, it seems slightly brighter.

It is this sense of brightness with a feeling of calm that I use as my guide. If I only had my thoughts or my emotions to go on, there is no way I could reach any kind of decision because they are in disarray. Only the gentle assurance in my gut cuts through all the madness. And science backs this up. Our gut has many more neurons than our brain, so it is better equipped to consider important issues. That fact still blows my mind. (And, I guess that proves the point I'm making here.)

One decision-making skill I often use is reverse-engineering the options by imagining the outcome that brings the most peace and working backwards to see which decision my gut says will get me there. As we talked about in *Fork In The Road Moments*, this may be, on appearance, the hardest and most unlikely path. It is a process of learning to trust because, at first, it takes a measure of faith. I dared to trust my gut the first time, having no better option. And when I could see it served me, I tried it again, and again. In time, it has become my sixth sense, and it never fails me.

Clare and I moved from her parents six months after we let go of the flat we had been accepted for because our individual and collective guts were telling us it was the right decision to make. It was during the first UK Covid-19 lockdown when nobody knew how bad the pandemic was or what the rules were about moving. Most people were not moving because of fear and cautiousness, so the market was wide open.

One issue we faced was the way the benefits system works in this country. You have to move and then apply for the housing element once you are there. This felt like a massive risk. To commit to moving, move all our stuff in and potentially find out we weren't eligible for support. We went with our guts and it paid off big time.

Gut instincts are not always the best way to make decisions. It is not appropriate to look to your gut for whether to look after your child today, or pay your bills. More often than not, you don't need your gut to decide whether you should evacuate a burning building. Also, where best practices exist, it is usually best to go with them. That doesn't mean that you should ignore your gut in these situations, but that it may not be the best or the only thing to consider.

In matters of the heart and life direction, your gut will serve you well if you can learn to hear it.

Wearing Different Hats

As we get ready to move into the next section, which focuses on the deep work, I want to talk about some of the different roles you'll play during this process. We've already covered *Surveyor* and *Architect* in the preparation phase and now we're going to look at the more hands-on roles. You're going to take the role of *builder* at some point and *interior designer* at others. Plus, many other roles.

I'm going to highlight now the two that I think are most important.

Safety Inspector

First on site is the *Safety Inspector*. In recent years, in the UK and many other countries, health and safety has become so extreme that there is a rule for everything. I've worked on many building sites in different roles and it is maddening to have to weigh up every decision and know that you are being scrutinised by people with beady eyes whose job it is to pick faults in your work process.

One place where I worked as a cleaner was the most extreme on health and safety. On my first day, I took a call on the phone and almost immediately a guy stopped me and said, "Can you please stand still while you're on the phone?" I said, "You're kidding, right?" And he looked at me gravely. "No", he said. In time, I came to learn that everything had a rule in that place. 'Walk on the left and hold the handrail, up and down the stairs.' 'No stopping to talk to anyone on the stairs,' etc.

And, in my cleaning role, I had to make sure wet floor signs were visible at each end of every section of the massive corridor where people were walking when cleaning the floor. There weren't enough signs to cover the entire length of the corridor because it was so big. So, it meant going back and getting signs from the first section where it had (hopefully) dried. If I failed to do this properly, it was seconds before someone pointed it out. The last one I understood, but the others seemed like overkill.

And some people there took great pleasure in being the 'teacher's pet'. One guy reported me because I paused on the stairs to say to a colleague that I couldn't talk to them while on the stairs, so I'd go down and come back up. The guy was happy he'd caught me. There was a reward for snitching.

This all seemed like a waste of time to me. Until I learnt the thinking behind it. The facility, of many hundreds of people, had not had an incident of any kind in nearly a year. A sister site just a few miles away had a clean sheet of only a few weeks and one incident was someone slipping down the stairs and breaking their neck because they weren't holding the handrail.

So, although it feels patronising to be told to hold the handrail while walking up and down the stairs, everything seems different when you realise the actual motivation behind it. It's either 'lots of petty rules' or 'potentially life-saving measures'.

So, what's the relevance?

Deep work can only proceed if it's safe to do so. Your brain is governing that. And it's your role as *Safety Inspector* to ensure it is adhered to. Never try to force the process because it is never safe to do so.

I've been having new memories of abuse come back as I've been writing this section. As one of my friends pointed out to me recently, the memories are surfacing now because I have got to a place where I'm strong enough and in a safe enough position for them not to destroy me. This is the safety mechanism at work to protect me.

During my 2019 crisis, I did something that went against everything in my being at that point. In the middle of the night, I phoned the local crisis team while in full flashback and very drunk. The kind stranger at the end of the phone helped me come out of flashback and to a place where I felt safe enough to go to bed. The next evening, having completely forgotten the whole thing, there was a knock at the door, and when Clare answered, there were two angels – her words – who had come to check on me. I had apparently arranged for them to come on the phone the night before.

The reason it was against everything in me to ring that crisis line is because I never want to be seen as weak. I want to stand on my own two feet. I want to 'be a man'. But, I recognised at that moment that I was on the edge of taking my own life and could see the toll it was having on Clare and her parents.

The other major reason I didn't want to call is because I had trusted similar services many times for over 20 years and they had almost all let me down. I had never got the help before, so why would I get it now? As understandable as this thinking is, when it's life or death, it can't be the deciding factor.

If you need help, you need help. Put your *Safety Inspector* hat on whenever you notice something that could cause you or anyone else harm. Assess the situation. And take the appropriate action to ensure your and others' safety.

Project Manager

The major role of the *Project Manager* is to oversee the entire process and orchestrate the different parts so that every part of the process works together in harmony. You also need to know what is within your capabilities and the capabilities of your team to make sure things are moving at the right pace and according to plan.

"But, I don't know how to do that," you say. That's not a problem because it's something you can learn as you go.

With your *Project Manager* hat on, you are in charge of the entire process and every other role must listen to what you have to say. Often, a Project Manager is working for a client who can overrule them, but in this case, that's you. So, hopefully, as you learn to work in harmony with yourself, it'll all go smoothly, seeing as each part of you wants the same successful outcome.

Your life project of building your superstructure is more complex than any physical building. It will take everything in you to navigate all the distractions, pitfalls, holdups, attacks, collapses, and everything else life throws at you. But, if you learn to live in the *now*, let peace be your guide, and take your time at those fork-in-the-road moments, you'll learn the skills needed to see the build through to completion.

Your role as *Project Manager* is yours and yours alone. It is possible to give up this role and allow other people to take charge, but then you're going to end up with a life that essentially belongs to other people and reflects them. However, if you want that dream life, you need to take charge and make the hard decisions to keep your life project on track.

When I look back over my 22-year journey of trying to get my life on track, it is easy to see the progression and how what I needed along the way always presented itself once I was ready. But, if I just think about where I started from, it's hard to believe that I ever made it past the first year. If I look closely, I can see points where I put on my *Project Manager* hat, took control of myself, and declared to the world, "This superstructure is getting built!"

You can do this too. I believe in you!

Assemble the Rest of Your Team

Even though you must play different roles in this process, that doesn't mean you don't need other people.

As appealing as it can be to stand alone, no person is an island. We need each other.

This is hard to accept if you don't feel that other people have proven themselves trustworthy, and if each time you dare to trust, you get hurt again. I completely understand this and empathise. But without other people, you will not get to where you want to be. You'll get so far on your own, but not all the way.

That being said, deciding who to have in your team is a big deal.

For me, the most helpful thing in coming to terms with needing other people was facing this reality: there's no such thing as a self-made person. Someone else fed you, bathed you, and wiped your butt for the first years of your life. You learnt to speak from the people around you. Every concept in your head originated from somebody else. You like the things that you like because of the people that you resonate with the most.

If, like me, you devote your life to learning, you will learn everything you learn from others – from people that have (hopefully) walked the walk that you want to walk, so they can now talk the talk. We are all like we are because of other people.

Thanks to the internet, the first people I surrounded myself with at the beginning of my process were people that I would have had no access to without it. I searched out the people who were successful, according to my measure of what success was, and learned from them. This is a good way to overcome the feeling that no one is safe or trustworthy. You can keep your distance without them knowing you exist and still make them part of your team.

133

But, when it comes down to it, you're going to need actual human beings in your life too:

Family

If your family is supportive and safe, then that's great. But, if every time you have contact with them it's destructive, you need to consider whether you should cut off or limit contact with them. Or, maybe space from each other for a time will help to resolve the underlying issues. I know that, to some people, this is an outrageous concept. Family is family. I get that. But once we are adults, if another person can't respect us as an adult, then something has to change. Sometimes, this takes drastic action.

My relationship with my mum was very confusing for many years because I had to rely on her for everything, even after I'd become an adult in the eyes of the law. From her point of view, I was incapable of looking after myself and understandably so. I was a complete mess. In my mid-20s, I had been to rehab for a couple of years and although I mostly stopped taking all hard drugs, I was drinking harder than I had before rehab. One night in my room, my gut suddenly told me I should move to Exeter and gain my independence. Even though it seemed a ridiculous idea because I was in such a mess and unable to look after myself, it came with that sense of peace that we talked about earlier.

I had to fight to make my move to Exeter happen because I was so all over the place. But I saw that the co-dependent and enabling relationships with my family, especially my mum, meant I would never get free in that environment. I had to get out of there. Once I left, I deliberately didn't get in contact for a while and had to establish some really hard boundaries. My mum had strong preconceptions about how things should be between us – every parent struggles with letting their children go.

Things went downhill massively over the next couple of years in Exeter, which could have suggested I'd made a poor decision by moving. But I had my *Project Manager* hat on and was learning the ropes. Exeter turned out to be my proving ground, where I found my way gradually forward without the pressure and influence of my family. And that eventually led me here.

Fast forward a few years, and I now have a great relationship with all my family. They are on my team. I speak with them regularly because I like them and enjoy their company. This is possible because we are all treating each other like adults and respect each other's time, space, ideas, values. It is hard-earned, but it is so worth it. They all truly feel like my family now and I know they love me and have my back. The hard decisions I made along the way that seemed so brutal and even unkind, feel so worth it now because I have a family.

I know that this may not be possible for you, and if that's the case, I'm really sorry. But, if your biological or adoptive family can't be your family, there's a world of people who can be your friends *and* your family.

Friends

Friends take many forms. We say we like people for many reasons, but most friendships are born out of a shared situation – same school, same hockey club, same concert. We are friends with people because we resonate with them and because we share something in common, even if we are actually very different people.

Parting ways with friends can be as hard as with family, especially if they were BFFs (Best Friends Forever). But, as you go through this process, you may find, as I did, that you slowly grow apart from some people. With some friends, this will just happen slowly and naturally until it fizzles out, but with others, you may find that it causes confusion and conflict.

Just like with dating, often, the kindest thing to do is to let someone down gently by telling them the truth. They may not understand or like it at all, but at least they'll know where they stand with you.

I went through many years where the only people I saw were my oldest and best friends. And I only saw them when I had the energy and felt strong enough to handle it. Even my closest friends could derail me without meaning to because I was so fragile. So, I had to be really careful.

One of my best friends, George, is one of my newest friends. He has really been there for me over the last few years. He's supported and believed in me through very messy times. And listened to me endlessly talk about my dreams, even though there was hardly any evidence to point to. I don't know where I would be without him. Making one new friend who truly has your back could be the difference between making it or not.

Unlike your family, there are millions of potential friends in this world. As scary and challenging as it might be to find them, it's worth the effort. Do everything you can to find like-minded, like-hearted people who have your best interests at heart. People who will support you while you go through this process, and believe in you when you're down in the deep mucky hole with no sign of anything happening above ground for years at a time.

Everyone needs friends like that.

Mentors

Mentors can be pretty much anyone who can support, advise, or guide you in a particular area of your life, or in life in general. They are often someone who has walked the path you want to walk, which means they can help you navigate the obstacles you'll face and give you wisdom on how to avoid the pitfalls they fell into. They can also help with accountability.

Whereas a coach will usually help you achieve specific goals with a structured process and outcome, a mentor is alongside you to offer support and encourage you. A coach may come to you with a specific method for you to follow, whereas a mentor should work with your way of doing things and not push their agenda on you.

It is unnecessary for them to be a million miles ahead of you. I've heard of people who have asked a friend who is just a few months ahead in a particular learning process to mentor them.

I have worked with both coaches and mentors. For this life process, I recommend finding mentors rather than coaches – people you can add to your team who have gone through a similar experience and come out the other side, having achieved their goals. They don't have to be someone you actually know. They don't even have to be alive (not talking séance here). You can read the literature of strangers who died hundreds of years ago and they can mentor you through their process, saving you potentially years of unnecessary struggle.

I have had many mentors and coaches in different areas. In terms of mentors, I have had formal situations where I paid for the privilege, and friends who are older that I wanted to emulate. I have also learnt from people I've discovered online whose teachings I've devoured without ever contacting them.

A few things I learnt:

1. Nothing has catapulted my learning more than having mentors. There is no replacement for the life wisdom that someone can share who has already lived the life you want to live.
2. In my early years, I got taken in by people who were con artists or whose primary motivation was money. I hadn't yet learnt to determine who was really on my side or not. This is best avoided, but it has taught me who not to trust. There's a lot of them out there.
3. Some mentors I had were giving brilliant advice for the time when they were at the top of their game, but not so much anymore. This was mainly in business but applies to all of life. While there are some principles that don't change with time, there are others that

become obsolete in a few short years as the world and our understanding about life develops and changes. An example in terms of below-ground learning is the difference between what a mental health worker would have advised 10 years ago versus now.

4. Some mentors may want you to agree with them *because* they've already succeeded and think they know better. This is hard to navigate from a position of relative ignorance. However, no matter how knowledgeable and successful a person is, you must never give them your *Project Manager* hat. You are the one in charge, and you must make every decision for yourself.

5. If you're paying your mentor, make sure they're not bigging you up because you are paying their bills with your monthly fee. Look for feedback elsewhere from people who will tell you if you're barking up the wrong tree or your idea isn't that good.

6. Some mentors had built what I wanted to build in one area (business, music) but had never struggled in the way I had (mental health, addiction). They couldn't conceive of anything other than simply making things happen and overcoming whatever stood in their path. This meant I felt like I had to hide my struggles from them. Not a healthy or beneficial relationship. And not fair to them because I wasn't trusting them or giving them the entire picture.

7. Despite all the potential pitfalls when finding a mentor, nothing has helped me more than to have someone come with me through the processes of life and offer their help and support. I highly recommend finding one.

Filling in Where There are Gaps

You are unlikely to build a team that is complete. You may be in a position where you don't have anyone, or don't know how to trust anyone. In either case, you can fill those roles yourself until you are in a better position.

I have mentored myself by imagining what a kind uncle-type would advise me. I have learnt to re-parent myself as a way of healing from my childhood abuse and neglect. And, when I couldn't trust anyone, I learnt to trust myself and be the best friend I could be to myself. I know these concepts may sound weird. They did to me when I first encountered them. But the alternative is potentially languishing in a sea of loneliness and non-productivity.

Build a team that can support you as you build your dream life.

Get your spade ready, it's digging time.

DIG DOWN DEEP

17

YOUR QUEST FOR STABILITY
Becoming Whole One Day at a Time

You're making progress.

You can actually see things improving now.

You feel you're nailing a lot of the roles you need to play. And getting comfortable being *Project Manager*. You don't shy away from the tough decisions like you used to.

You've surrounded yourself with good people who understand what you're aiming for and they've committed to supporting you.

There's no question in your mind now that you need to stick with the process for the long haul, but you still have questions.

What does digging deep really look like?

What am I actually aiming for internally?

How will I know when I'm done?

You're looking for reassurance.

Structural Integrity

I get that, and I want to help to make things easier.

This process is all about structural integrity. And, whether your life thrives or collapses is all down to how sound your foundation is.

Brené Brown says it like this:

**"Integrity is choosing courage over comfort;
choosing what is right over what is fun, fast, or easy;
and choosing to practice our values rather than simply professing
them."** [29]

Martha Beck, author of *The Way of Integrity: Finding the path to your
true self,* says:

**"Peace is your home, integrity is the way to it,
and everything you long for will meet you there."**[30]

Without structural integrity, even the strongest and most beautifully built buildings will collapse in on themselves.

When we reach a point of crisis, the natural response may be to look outside ourselves for answers. And, more than likely, people will try to correct the visible issues, which may actually be just a symptom of an underlying and deep-rooted problem. A well-meaning manager sees that you're very stressed at work and suggests taking a long weekend next month to recover. Or, a friend, noticing your low mood, suggests keeping a gratitude diary for a month.

The issue with these suggestions is not that they have no merit, it's just that, if there is a hidden structural issue, it's more like putting a plaster on a skin ulcer when the cause is diabetes, or putting a rug over a sinkhole in your living room. If the foundation is strong enough, a force 10 storm will not touch the building. If the foundation has collapsed, a sneeze could bring the whole thing crashing down.

[29] Brene Brown. *Rising Strong*. 1st ed. (London, GB, VERMILION, 2015.)

[30] McKenzie Jean-Philippe. 'Martha Beck Speaks On How to "Stop Pushing Back" Against Fate'. Oprah Daily, Oprah Daily LLC, 2021,
www.oprahdaily.com/life/relationships-love/a36078639/martha-beck-quotes.

When I was growing up, I would get so desperate about what I faced that I would seek out anyone I thought could help me and give advice on what to do. In response to sharing with these people about my addictions, flashbacks, depression and suicidal thoughts, the usual advice was essentially, "Try harder, create a routine, get up earlier, read the bible/pray more, think about others." These were the kinder suggestions.

The least kind and most unhelpful were more like the, "You're lazy and have an excuse for everything," I mentioned earlier. Now, I don't doubt the advice worked to an extent for the advice-givers with their struggles. But no matter how hard I tried to make it work, I would end up back in what felt like exactly the same place.

Why? What was wrong with me? Well, for a start, the actual answer lay in understanding 'What *happened* to me?' And also, "What wasn't I given that these advice-givers were?" They were advising me according to their paradigm and didn't take the time to find out what mine was – before sharing their 'wisdom'. And, because their paradigm was something like 'just get on with it' and 'make the best of a bad situation', that's the best they could offer.

This is the reason I suggest many times in this book to seek professional help if you can. They are (usually) the best people to advise you on your complex and deep-seated issues. They can do it from a position that is non-judgmental since they are not personally involved or affected by the things you face. And they should understand that the individuals who seem the most sorted and together may actually be the most vulnerable and close to crisis.

Those who are not trained and don't spend their time considering the complexities of humanity tend to offer simplisms instead of actual wisdom. The reason being, their way works for them and seems like such a simple solution to them, therefore, it must work for you too (and everybody else). It takes a lot of effort and time to see different points of view and imagine what life is really like for other people. Also, I've discovered that if you do make the effort to understand someone else, it can be really painful, which is another reason people live on the surface of life. It's just too big an investment.

Growing up, one of my biggest issues was that I'd developed a persona based on approval from the tribe, which led to me being incapable of showing what was really going on inside me. For those not trained to see behind my convincing veneer (and even some that were), I seemed like a friendly, cheerful, intelligent, strong young man. And that's all they saw. Dig down even a few inches and it was a very different story.

Everything I'm talking about here will resonate with some aspects – or all – of your life. When you did *Your Structural Survey*, it will have revealed some areas that are unsupported and in need of attention. Focussing your time and attention in these areas is what's going to bring about lasting change.

I am an idealist at heart, even though the things I've suffered have forced me to view life from other standpoints. With my idealist hat on, I believe that one of the biggest solutions to many of the world's problems is for us all to live from a place of integrity – true to ourselves. If every person was at ease with themselves and only did what was in their heart to do, refusing what was not, peace would be the default state. The world would not be problem-free, but a world full of people living from a place of integrity is the closest thing to paradise that I can imagine.

However, most people are looking outside themselves to get their answers, so there is a constant feedback loop that regurgitates the same old same old. When even one person dares to look inwards and live from a place of integrity, they can disrupt the status quo and elevate the entire world's position.

When starting out, it can be very hard to determine which parts of you are really you and which parts have developed in response to trauma and the need to survive. I thought I was a tough guy for many years because part of me *had* become very tough to protect myself against further abuse and pain. Over the years, I learned about another side of me, which is soft and caring. It's taken me years to get to where I can access that part of me and admit it to myself to write the kinds of things I'm writing here. It's vulnerable and sometimes scary. But if I don't show the integrity I'm promoting, then I'm a fraud and can't help anyone.

Finding and repairing the parts of your deep life that lack integrity is one of the most important things you'll ever do.

Make it your lifelong habit to turn inwards and do that work.

Why Dig Deep?

"Just leave well enough alone." "You're overthinking things." "If it ain't broke, don't fix it."

I understand these objections completely.

Despite the years I've spent in this process, I truly wish things were different. If there was any way to avoid facing up to what's inside, I probably still would. But when there is even a tiny fracture in your structural integrity, things *are* 'broke' and they *do* need fixing! This is true despite the facade looking shiny. We must get to the heart of where issues lie in order to make them a thing of the past.

Digging deep is scary as hell. It will take immense courage. But it is absolutely necessary.

Resting Your Way to Success

Digging deep is the hardest work you'll ever do. I have done many backbreaking manual labour jobs and none of them compare with how hard internal work can be. The funny thing is, you can do some of the hardest graft internally while lying absolutely motionless in your bed, as I have countless times. It requires no external effort whatsoever to make this heart-process work. That doesn't mean it's not exhausting though because there is still a great deal of energy involved. For me, the energy required is more than shifting a tonne of rocks in searing heat. Likewise, the reward is greater.

There are some things you can't build or fight your way out of. For years, I would try harder and harder again, thinking that trying harder was enough to bring success, just like the 'wise' people had persuaded me to do. But this precipitated my chronic fatigue. My first major 'crash', where I could no longer push past my exhaustion, came after a solo charity bike ride to raise money for a water pump in a village in Africa. I woke up the morning of the ride with nothing in me to get out of bed. Two nights before, I had been out the whole night drinking with no recollection of the night or how I got home. I was still feeling the effects. The bike ride was from Windsor Castle to Exeter Castle, which is 150 miles. By 60 miles, I was done and consciously had to turn each leg one after the other. I was hanging over the handlebars. By 100 miles, I was thinking about how long it would be before the ambulance arrived to cart me off to hospital. Through grit and determination, I stuck it out and beat my 12-hour aim by just minutes.

On one level, that's a great achievement, but I'm not sharing it for that reason. I'm sharing it because it sums up my entire lifetime of trying harder to solve problems. A few weeks later, I was in my first flat. I'd just left the voluntary youth work position which I worked at for a few years. It had been relentless. On the weeks we organised for kids, we would start at 7 am and go through till 11 pm most days. So, to train for the bike ride, my alarm went off at 3 am and I trained until 5 am. I drank literally litres of coffee to keep me going. And ate packets of biscuits a day for the sugar hit.

I woke up on the first morning in that new flat and couldn't get out of bed. There was nothing left in the tank. I spent the next few weeks in bed with the curtains closed. My younger sister had to come over and clean up. There was mould growing on the pile of dirty washing up.

147

This was just the first crash. There were many more in my journey of learning to look for the answers inside myself – rather than pushing on, expecting different results.

This pushing on regardless is a trait I learnt from observing my mum. And it's so ingrained, I still face it daily. I have to force myself to take breaks and take days off because part of me still genuinely believes that I must use every second or I'm going to fail. My mum is also still learning similar lessons.

Over time, I have learnt that I can often achieve more by doing nothing externally and turning all my attention inwards to face an internal problem head-on. I call this, *resting my way to success*. When I've talked to some people about this, they respond with massive resistance because it challenges their sense of how someone ought to be as an adult.

They think you should always be busy contributing, hardworking, etc. But what they can't understand is that I'm not trying to sell some new-fangled idealism. I'm talking about a strategy that could be the difference between life or death, success or failure. And I take that extremely seriously.

My dad died when he was 45 from a massive heart attack that was brought on by a very stressful situation he was facing. He had struggled throughout his entire life and never got unstuck, being unable to see on his own what needed to change. He was often furious and violent towards me and my mum, and extremely controlling as well. In the year before he died, he started to change. One of my only memories from growing up is walking in on him crying in his bedroom and asking him what was wrong. He was getting beneath the veneer. But it was too late to turn his life around in time to save himself.

After that, there were multiple occasions where it looked like we could lose my mum as well, culminating in a lymphoma diagnosis in 2007. It came during some of my worst years when I'd left home for the first time, at 25. I had recently lost my benefits because of an unfair medical assessment that judged me based on appearances. As I've said, this never reflected my struggles. This forced me to get a job but I felt so incapable of even starting there. I drank and took cocaine the whole of the night before my first day. I somehow made it to work with no sleep and made it through the whole day. As a manager trained me on a computer, *I* could smell the alcohol coming from my mouth and pores. So, unless I got the one person with zero sense of smell, he could too. But he said nothing.

My drinking soon made me homeless. I felt like such a failure and saw no hope whatsoever. I didn't know how to keep living and faced suicide every day. Every bridge I walked over, I felt the unbearable urge to throw myself off. I was experiencing near-constant panic attacks being outside. And, eventually, I decided I must end it all. This wasn't the first time. But this time, instead of overdosing, which is what I'd done before, I threw myself in a river, unable to swim. I was in a part of the city where there were not many people and it was dark as it was late at night. But someone passing by happened to see me and threw me a lifeline. And the police came and got me out.

As a policeman walked me away from the river, I kept saying, "I want to die. I want to die." The policeman said, "No, you don't," in a condescending tone. "If you really wanted to die," he said, "you wouldn't have grabbed the lifeline." It shocked me, and those words still hurt today. A part of me did want to die and have it all be over. But that didn't mean there wasn't another part fighting for my survival, which is why I reached for that lifeline. There was a glimmer of hope mixed with the unbearable feeling of what my death would do to my family, especially my nephews, who I adore. So, there *was* a part of me that hoped someone would find me and pull me out. But, as strong – or stronger – was the overriding image that played over and over of being swept away by the current and down the weir. To finally have peace. This level of confusion has been my experience every time I've felt close to suicide. And why would anyone expect any different from someone in that state?

The police put me in a cell for the night and when they notified the lady I was lodging with about what had happened to me, she said that I shouldn't be in a cell. I needed a hospital instead. They transported me to a ward at the nearest hospital where, a few hours later, someone from the mental health team assessed me and decided that I was OK to be released. I found this to be the case 99% of the time in those situations because the NHS was and is so overstretched. I'm not sure how much worse I needed to be to get help, but I didn't meet the mark on that occasion. It was always a surreal experience walking out of the hospital from these incidents and going about my life as though nothing had happened.

In the years after this, I thought that the suicide attempt was a consequence of losing my benefits and being made homeless. It wasn't until a few years ago that I read in my medical records my mum had received a cancer diagnosis just weeks before this incident. I was so dissociated from what I felt, I couldn't see the impact on me.

In 2010, while working at the youth work charity, my mum was living just down the road, so I would drop in on her from time to time. After two successful bouts of chemotherapy in 2009 and '10, she had become very unwell again.

I could see that my mum was giving up on everything and she just endlessly zoned out in front of the TV. I was angry – not at her, but at the injustice of what was happening to her – because I knew that was not how she wanted her life to be. So, I confronted her. "If you don't turn this rubbish off, stop ignoring what's going on with your body, and start looking at things, you're going to end up dead. Is that really what you want?" I hadn't learnt how to confront kindly yet and I was just trying with everything I had to persuade her to look inside and stop ignoring the things she was hiding from. I reminded her of her great desire to see her grandchildren grow up and see all her children get married. She was able to hear what I was trying to say and started the process of looking inside again. To this day, she talks about that tactless challenge as a major turning point for her.

The next year, I was on an aid trip to Nicaragua and felt like I should ring home. I rang my older sister, who I was still living with while at the youth work charity. When she answered her phone, she didn't sound surprised to hear from me, which was strange because I had never called her whilst being abroad before. It became clear she'd emailed me with news about my mum and she thought I was responding to the email. But the email had never got through.

She said mum's leukaemia had suddenly become high grade, and she had been rushed by ambulance to hospital with sepsis, pleurisy, and had gone into renal failure, which meant she would need dialysis for the rest of her life. The dialysis didn't work at first and she could not have the planned spleen removal or chemotherapy because she was too unwell. The consultant repeated that it didn't look good, and she didn't have much longer left.

I had to decide whether to stay or return. I went with my gut and stayed. From what my sister had said, I probably wouldn't make it back in time to be there to say goodbye and I wanted to make the most of the good thing that I was part of in Nicaragua and not cut it short. But, more than that, I wanted to believe that despite the consultant's verdict, she would pull through somehow.[31]

Later on in my trip, when I next spoke with my sister, she told me that my mum had improved, and the consultant kept calling it a miracle. She was off dialysis and well enough to start chemotherapy. She was going to pull through. Again.

When I finally made it to the hospital on my return, my mum was still in a bad way but appeared almost elated. She explained she'd had a near-death experience and that she'd drawn a line in the sand (which she had actually done in the jelly in the bowl in front of her), saying that her life

---

[31] Looking back on this, I find it hard to believe I didn't get on the next plane back. But, that is where I was at that point. If it were now, nothing could stop me from getting back as fast as I could.

was going to be different going forward. She was saying 'no more' to the way things had been.

A few months ago, my mum faced the news that she had breast cancer and the lymphoma was still present. She went through surgery plus radiotherapy and oral chemotherapy to tackle it head-on. Until a few weeks ago, she had continual infections and couldn't do anything much at all, so feared the worst. But at her next appointment with the specialist, all the results were stable, so she just needs to continue to be monitored. Recently, she seems the best she has for a long time.

I share all these stories for a few reasons. The first is to show where my motivation comes from to do whatever it takes to remain alive and healthy. As much as it's in my power, I don't want my life to be cut short or consumed with sickness and endless struggles. And, I want to overcome the things my parents weren't able to because I want a life worth living. The second reason is that although we rightly esteem people who survive their struggles with cancer and similar illnesses, there is something in my mum's story that is unexpected, which I left out just now.

My mum's recovery was not because she *fought* the cancer. What actually happened when she drew that line in the jelly and said, 'No more,' was that she gave up – not on life, but *for* life. She stopped fighting and let go of everything, experiencing a peace and rest in that moment like nothing else she'd ever known. Then followed an assurance that she was going to be OK.

This concept of 'letting go' is one of the earliest concepts I got hold of. It is so deeply integral to this process that, for years, it was my answer to everything. I still regularly respond to Clare with, "Face it and let it go," when she asks, "What shall I do?" about something that's stuck in her life. It is not always a helpful answer, but more often than not, it is what needs to happen at some point.

The origins and basic meaning of 'forgiveness' is simply 'letting go'. Religion has made it about the other person but it is just about ourselves. Holding onto something to punish another has no effect on them. It only hurts us. To really live, we must let it all go. Not out of obligation to God or duty to other people but out of kindness to ourselves and only when *we* are ready.

My mum came to that place of letting go completely in that hospital bed when she drew that line in the jelly. She forgave (let go of) everything. And the results were miraculous. Even reversing the destructive effects of the cancer, which appeared to be irreversible. My theory for why those miraculous effects occurred is because when she let go of everything in that moment, she released all the stress from her body. My brother-in-law visited my mum at the hospital when she was at her worst and also soon after she drew that line and let go. He said it was like visiting two different people. Before, she was how you'd expect someone gravely ill to seem, and after, she was the happiest he'd ever seen her.

Stress is accepted by medicine and science to be a major cause of most illnesses. And stress is one of the major consequences of experiencing trauma. *The Body Keeps The Score*, an exceptional book by Bessel van der Kolk about the lasting effects of trauma on our bodies, details how childhood trauma can predict adult illness, even down to what the type of illness will be.[32]

There is a test called the ACE test[33] (Adverse Childhood Experiences) which has 10 questions relating to abuse, neglect, and family dysfunction. The higher your score, the higher the likelihood that you will develop health problems in later life. A score of 4 or more is serious. I score 9/10. I can fill a few pages with the illnesses and various symptoms I've experienced, including some that are very serious. For me, the connection between upbringing and health in later life is clear.

---

[32] Bessel van der Kolk, MD. *The Body Keeps The Score*. 1st ed. (Penguin, 2015.)

[33] Laura Starecheski. 'Take The ACE Quiz – And Learn What It Does And Doesn't Mean'. Npr, 2015, www.npr.org/sections/health-shots/2015/03/02/387007941/take-the-ace-quiz-and-learn-what-it-does-and-doesnt-mean.

A lot of what we experience in our bodies is like a warning light trying to get us to look deeper. The big 'C' word – cancer – fills people with fear. 'One in two of us will get…' But what if cancer is not the thing that we should really fear? What if there is something much bigger beneath the surface? Well, my mum's story says that, for her, there was. Over the next 10 years, she gradually made sense of why her life had been like it had and understood what led her to her deathbed.

It was the principle and practice of rest that has got her from that point to this. What happened to my mum in that hospital bed was described as a miracle by a medical consultant. Meaning, unexplainable by medical science. It makes no sense. It doesn't happen. When your body is in that state, it's days or hours. That's it, no exceptions.

Except… it turns out there are.

I can't prove what happened. I can't convince you if you don't believe it. It takes a measure of faith. But that is what happened, and for my mum, her recovery resulted from that letting go.

Resting your way to success is not an airy-fairy, wishy-washy idealism. It is a potentially lifesaving strategy to navigate the effects of trauma and keep you here on this earth. It doesn't require external effort using physical strength. But it will require everything you have to learn and master.

I highly recommend rest as part of your strategy for success.

Stripping Back the Layers

As we learn to dig deep, there is a progressive process of stripping back the layers that have formed over time. As we peel back the carpet in our superstructure, it reveals lino, which, in turn, reveals hardwood floor, which was laid over a concrete foundation. Each layer represents a timeframe in our lives. Without getting beneath these layers, there can be no structural work. And we can't get a proper view of what's down there without peeling it all back.

Stripping back the layers is rarely appealing and never easy. But it is one of the best investments you can make for your life. If you are met with internal resistance, it's worth asking why. Maybe a part of you knows that you're going to discover something you'd rather not remember or have to face up to.

As I wrote above about my mum's near-death experience, I had two realisations[34] [35] that result from stripping back the layers as I've honestly told my story. How could I not realise until 40 years old that coming to terms with the possibility of being an adult orphan at 30 may have had something to do with my 'crash' a couple of weeks later? The answer is: because it was just too painful. And that's what we're all trying to avoid. The pain of life that we really know is lying just beneath the surface.

The snapshots I've shared are the story of my whole life. I don't really need to go into much more detail for you to understand my life because each story will be much like the next. An endless cycle of struggle and crisis moments. Except that, in the end, it wasn't endless. And, the reason is that I got started with the process at 18 years old, stripping back the layers and grappling with why my life was the way it was. From that point, the process took 20 years to produce the results I was craving. Ouch. That really hurts. At times, it's unbearable. But, the alternatives were premature death, as it was for my dad and a lot of my friends. Or many years on the fringes of death, like my mum.

---

[34] I only just realised as I was writing that 2011 was also the year that I decided to try and spend six months in the wilderness. It's where my journey of rest began. I think I saw how futile my mum's journey of always pushing on had been. Her recent brush with death was a motivator for me, as was the powerful effect that resting and letting go had on her entire being.

[35] I've also only just realised that soon after coming back from Nicaragua, I did the 150-mile bike ride and my body 'crashed' for the first time, putting me in bed for a few weeks. I'm not sure I ever correlated my 'crash' with my mum nearly dying. Wow, I've still got a lot to learn about myself.

I want more. I want better. I crave a long life full of good things. Nothing has ever fully extinguished that fire.

The objections from the opening of this chapter are all things people have said to me. Such is the aversion to looking inside and peeling back the layers. I'm sure you'll encounter these and similar ideas from others along the way, and if you do, and you start to feel unsure of yourself and this process, just ask: what is so bad about wanting to spend time with yourself? You spend time with people that you want to get to know and become comfortable around. You spend time with people to resolve issues that have formed between you. There is no other way. So, what is strange about doing that with yourself? I'd say, 'nothing'. In fact, if you want to feel at ease with yourself, there is no other way.

I have total respect for anyone that commits to this process. There are some physical feats I am in awe of, but none of them require the courage that you must show to get beneath life's veneer and get real.

Stripping back the layers uncovered every single aspect of my life that was keeping me stuck and broken. And it revealed the steps required to reach this life I now love.

That's what I'm inviting you to be part of.

Essentialism

In his book, *Essentialism: The Disciplined Pursuit of Less*, Greg McKeown says:

"Essentialism is not about how to get more things done; it's about how to get the right things done. It doesn't mean just doing less for the sake of less either. It is about making the wisest possible investment of your time and energy in order to operate at our highest point of contribution by doing only what is essential."[36]

---

[36] Greg McKeown. *Essentialism: The Disciplined Pursuit of Less*. 15th ed., (Virgin Books, 2021)

This is one of my favourite books and I'm sure I'll probably return to it throughout my life. Now, more than ever, in our fast-paced, always-busy world, we need to know what to focus our attention and energy on to escape the tyranny of urgency. Essentialism makes this a whole lot easier. Not to be confused with minimalism, which seeks to live with as little as possible, we can describe essentialism as 'just enough', meaning *just enough* of the right things. For one person, that *may* look like minimalism because that is their *just enough*, but for another, it might look like opulence.

Essentialism is not just about things. It is about every single aspect of life. *Just enough* of the right friends. *Just enough* of the right time spent on *just* the right tasks. And so on.

In deciding which opportunities to go for, or not, Warren Buffett says:

"The difference between successful people and really successful people is that
really successful people say no to almost everything."[37]

If your default is to please everyone, this is a hard thing to learn and you will meet with resistance from the tribe. But, one of the most important essentialist traits you can learn is to say 'no' as your default. So, if it's not a resounding 'yes' from your heart, in line with your values and 10-year plan, then it's a firm 'no'. There's no way to serve your plan and everyone else's at the same time. The world doesn't need you to do that. The world needs you to become the best version of yourself and create the greatest value *you* can give. That's what they're waiting for.

There will be times when you realise that you've committed to something and need to backtrack. The first time I did this was for a charity event that I had agreed to perform at. True to form, not only did I agree to sing

---

[37] Amy Blaschka. 'This Is Why Saying "No" Is The Best Way To Grow Your Career – And How To Do It'. Forbes, 2019, www.forbes.com/sites/amyblaschka/2019/11/26/this-is-why-saying-no-is-the-best-way-to-grow-your-career-and-how-to-do-it/?sh=75d96f77479d.

my songs accompanied by my guitar, I also further volunteered to create the flyers to advertise the event, plus a couple of other jobs. My drive to please others was strong.

I was really unwell at the time and was heading towards another 'crash', so I decided that, out of principle, I needed to pull out of the whole thing. I could have just stripped it back and done only what I could do on my laptop. But I wanted to see if the world would really fall apart if I went the whole hog. So, I explained to my friend that I needed to pull out for health reasons. He understood and was able to arrange for someone to take care of all the parts I was meant to be doing. It was my first lesson in realising not everything depends on me.

Over time, doing this has become easier and easier, and no matter what it feels like, you are rarely ever the only person who can do a particular thing. Or, if you are, it doesn't mean the whole thing is ruined because you're not there. Essentialism provides the way for you to be as kind and caring to yourself as you've felt obligated to be to other people.

After my 2011 'crash', my doctor signed me off from work, meaning I could receive social security. But I hated being in that position and would daily try to find ways to start providing for myself. I knew I couldn't work a job with my lack of energy, so I turned my attention to business. Unable to settle on what I wanted to do, I created a business card that had everything I could offer on it instead. I was a performer who could tidy up your garden and design your flyer, while fixing your computer, among other things… all at the same time. Not only is this jack-of-all-trades approach a poor strategy for the business and the customer, it is also a sure-fire way to spread yourself thin, burn yourself out, and fail to deliver value according to your greatest potential.

I soon realised the error in my approach and ditched everything that wasn't in line with my values and goals, which just left music-related offerings. Uncommitting from everything but the music elements meant I could help to build up a small music scene in the town where I was living, which I wouldn't have been part of if I had continued to spread myself so thin.

The reason I'm mentioning essentialism here is that there is no task more essential than digging deep to achieve structural integrity. There is no better use of your time and energy. As weeks turned into years in my process, I had to come to terms with the fact that it was going to be another few years before I saw the above-ground results I was looking for. Again and again, I had to get to where I could say, "If it takes another five or 10 years, I'm game." That's seriously hard. But I had no other viable option if I was ever going to reach my dream life. And the drive remained strong to get there.

It's only in the last few years, as I've lived the start of that dream life, that I can really see that it's been worth holding out for. If only I could've had that insight before getting started!

One of the biggest keys I've learnt to make life work is to strip everything back to leave only what's essential. From the outside, this could be mistaken for a life that is failing. But the exact opposite is true. It is a life that is in desperate measures to save what was worth saving and eliminate the unnecessary.

Greg McKeown, referencing Aristotle's view of the three different types of work – theoretical, practical, and poietical[38] – says:

"An Essentialist produces more – brings forth more – by removing more instead of doing more."[39]

Essentialism is a case where less truly is more.

My dad was a hoarder with a survivalist mentality. Not the kind that keeps a few useful items 'just in case', but the kind they make TV

---

[38] Wikipedia. 2021. "Poiesis." 14 November 2021. https://en.wikipedia.org/wiki/Poiesis
[39] Greg McKeown. *Essentialism: The Disciplined Pursuit of Less*. 15th ed. (Virgin Books, 2021)

programs about. After years of marriage, my parents and my two older siblings were living in a tiny two-bedroom cottage. My mum was expecting me at the time. My dad had filled the entire place top to bottom with his stuff in cardboard boxes and black bin liners. This was a nightmare for my mum. And with me on the way, she didn't know where she would put a cot for me to sleep in.

My mum got to the point where she had reached the limit of what she could take and said to my dad that she was leaving with the kids and not coming back until he'd cleared the cottage.

Two men from their church came to help my dad clear the cottage out. As my dad was picking up scraps of paper to read what each said and decide whether to keep them, the other two guys were slinging bags and boxes in the back of a huge trailer.

The two men and my dad transported everything they had cleared to a barn that belonged to one of the men. Once they had finished clearing, the entire barn was full with what had fitted into that tiny two-bedroom cottage.

When I was four years old, we moved to a bigger house as mum had just had my sister and we needed more space. Despite the massive clear out a few years before from the cottage, his remaining stuff still took up a great deal of space in the house. There were two attic rooms. My brother had one room, and the other was used to store the bulk of the boxes, which were floor to ceiling and wall to wall. I can remember creating a crawl space through the top layer of boxes just below the ceiling. It went all the way to the other side of the room and then dropped down next to a window where I used to hide and look out over the town.

My dad died a few years after we moved to that house. We didn't get rid of the last of his stuff until 20 years after when my mum finally left our family home. By that point, my brother and I were so sick of dealing with someone else's junk that when my mum was unsure what to do with an item, we'd just say, "Burn it," before even looking at what she was asking about. And if we could have, we would. Just before my mum moved, we found a charity shop that would take almost everything. We pulled up in a massive truck and finally got free of it all.

My brother and I both went to the other extreme from my dad and became minimalists. But I took it even further to the point of asceticism. I discovered there was no real virtue in this act because it achieves nothing if it is merely an attempt at an outside-inwards process and doesn't line up with your integrity. This is why I promote essentialism over minimalism.

Choose the way of essentialism for your life and make your heart your priority. Once your foundation is strong enough, you may look back and realise, like I can, that it was actually the fastest, most efficient way you could have gone about building your life while ensuring it remains.

Essentialism: The Disciplined Pursuit of Less, by Greg McKeown, is one of the books I highly recommend adding to your toolbox. It will give you more by giving you less:

Buy *Essentialism* here:

https://digdeepstandtall.com/get-essentialism-book
(Affiliate link)

Resonance

As our life comes into line with our integrity, we change not only in a way that we are aware of, but in a way that affects others as well.

You may have heard about the law of attraction. It is a very popular idea that you can attract anything to yourself by focusing on it. There are many spins on this idea from various religious and spiritual standpoints.

I spent a long time trying to *manifest* things into being and saw no results worth talking about. When I talked with those 'in the know' about where I was going wrong, they always suggested it was something I was doing, like not believing enough or, from the Christians, unacknowledged sin in my life.

The popular 'law' of attraction is based on the universal law of vibration. The physical law is actually called the law of resonance, which is secondary to the law of vibration.

The law of vibration states that everything in the universe is essentially energy and vibrates at different frequencies.
The law of resonance states that the rate of vibration projected will harmonise with and attract back energies with the same resonance. In other words, *like* attracts *like*.

Capitalising on these laws, there are those who have boiled it down to change your frequency by picturing, believing, and confessing positive things, and you will have what you want because it will attract *like* things into your life. I call this simplism and woo-woo because it is not trying to understand the complexity of how things work, but provides an easy 'hack' for people to latch onto. And you can't hack your heart (except maybe to pieces).

I'm not saying here that all hacks are bad. They are amazing when you're dealing with managing money or organising your sock drawer. Just not so much for the deeper life and your heart.

As I'll suggest later, all laws are universal laws and they are not really physical laws vs. spiritual laws. They are just universal laws that have an observable element and an unobservable element, but are all discernible.

Life is far more complex than any of us individually or collectively have been able to fathom so far. And I believe it takes a lot more than a shift in conscious thinking to get the results you want. At least, that's my experience.

That doesn't mean I don't believe that people *have* had success with these methods. But, if you've resonated (see what I did there) with what I've written in the book so far, they probably won't work for you. Why? Because I believe that resonance happens on a much deeper level than the level of conscious thought. And, because simply picturing something over and over and choosing to believe it will never touch the true blockages to us having the life that we really want.

The biggest blockages in my own life came because of trauma and its all-pervading effects. The things that happened to me when I was younger left no aspect of my life unscathed. This included my thoughts and imagination. My thoughts were horrific day and night. My imaginations were frightening and disturbed. So, I would listen to the advice of preachers and gurus and try to alter them from the outside in – believe harder, picture in as much detail as I could, and speak the 'truth' over and over like my life depended on it.

People who accused me of not trying hard enough didn't realise that I would practice this for days on end. One night, I stayed up until the sun came up to try to get rid of a migraine, which I suffered with frequently. I realised much later that a good night's sleep, or at least a night's rest, would have helped more.

The most extremely oppressive concepts of this came from certain religious people – one who said, "If Michael (my dad) wanted to be well, he would be." And when one such person asked me one morning how I was doing, I said, "Not too good, I'm feeling really unwell." I didn't get to finish the sentence because they jumped in with, "You mustn't say that, say, 'I'm blessed'."

Once I reached the place in life where I was strong enough to begin looking at the trauma I'd experienced, my entire life began changing a little at a time. I saw new possibilities when before all I saw was impossibility. I had moments where I'd catch myself thinking thoughts like "I actually like myself" as I glimpsed my reflection in a mirror. And I would hear words come out of my mouth that I would have never said, like, "I don't want to be addicted anymore. I want to change."

As amazing as these transformations are, they are just the symptom or the outcome of the deep work that was taking place in parts of me we can only understand with metaphors like 'heart' and 'soul'.

In time, I moved away and beyond everything I had believed up to that point, and discovered new people on the internet and in books that had messages that really excited me. I parted ways with some friends and grew closer to others. I see this as the law of vibration and resonance at work, but not in a way that I can package or easily understand.

My best way of putting it is that when we get to a point where our entire being resonates at the same frequency, we are in integrity, and we can have what we want almost effortlessly. It won't all come together overnight, but the process starts to happen with the first few structural changes.

I saw resonance work against me for many years in terms of who I drew to myself and situations I would end up in. I have many examples of this. But the example I come back to most often of resonance working against someone is a friend who, over the space of a few years, went from relationship to relationship where each partner abused her emotionally and physically. The men would start out lovely, and each time, she believed it would be different, but it always had the same ending.

I remember her getting together with one of these men she met in a club on a night out. After it went the same way as ever, I remember thinking, what was it that drew them to each other out of the hundreds of people there that night? I find it easy to imagine those guys were actually scoping out women who they could manipulate. But what about my friend? From what I know of her, she wasn't consciously going out looking for guys to beat her up. I think that type of relationship was the best she could imagine based on the way she felt about herself and what she had witnessed as a child between her parents. That's a simplistic answer, but I still believe it's true.

An example at the other extreme, from mine and Clare's life, is deciding where we wanted to live. We both independently loved Bath and said it was our favourite place early on. But we dismissed it because it didn't resonate with where we were at that point. We were all over the place and fractured within ourselves and had bought into the idea that Bath was too expensive. We didn't feel like we deserved it. And subconsciously, we felt like we needed to suffer more struggle and heartache. So, we bounced around from tough place to tough place, which on some level resonated with our low views of ourselves – views that came directly from trauma.

In November 2019, Clare and I were accepted for a flat in Bath. It was our dream come true. But my gut (not resonating with it) said we were at a fork in the road and going for it at that point would end in disaster. This came from the intuition that I was at the beginning of a major crisis because of what I'd remembered. We pulled out and let go of our dream. Again. A few days later, I was in full crisis and needed Clare and her parents' support all day, every day, to get through. Although it was unbearable to let the dream go once again, it meant that Clare wasn't on her own with me, drinking constantly and going missing every other day.

When the memories came back, I had just been promoted to *general manager* after only a few weeks as supervisor in a new job. I was on the best money I'd ever earned and they were talking about wanting me for *area manager* already. I learnt later that high-stress situations often bring on a crisis, which is when memories can come flooding back. My gut told me with all that was going on that if we moved to Bath, things would fall apart, and we would be stuck with a year's rental agreement on the flat with no way to pay it.

Everything my gut had reverberated with was proven right.

165

The amazing thing is that from the point of letting go of that flat to the point we got accepted for the next one was almost exactly six months. We had originally thought we would just get any place in Bath that we could find quickly and start looking for somewhere that was more permanent to rent until we bought. But after a while, we've decided we can happily stay where we are until we're ready to buy.

One of the biggest effects of a change of resonance is being able to notice things you would never have noticed before or accept things you couldn't accept before. This is partly because of apperception, which is making sense of new ideas by assimilation according to current ideas. I do this all the time with faces. I see new people and my mind says, 'They look like...' Similarly, if you are thinking about buying a green Volkswagen hatchback, you then see them everywhere. This is apperception at work. It applies in every area of our lives, including below-ground.

It is natural to see these laws from our own perspective in relation to other people and things. But the laws are working equally in the other direction as well, so it's hard to say who or what was the origin of a resonant outcome.

Clare and I had known each other for seven years, and then one day, I felt different about her. We had just been helping on the same youth work week where we met originally. After three days of churning over my feelings for her, I decided I had to tell her, even if it meant another failure and lost friend. I sent her a simple message and told her that my heart had changed towards her. She got back within a few hours and said that she had experienced the same thing. It was mutual, like everything good in a relationship is. Who changed first? I have no idea. But we resonated, and that drew us together.

The law of vibration is observable science and is a law in the entire universe, including our entire beings. As is the law of resonance. Like *does* attract like. If you want something to change in your life but every imagination, thought, and word out of your mouth is contrary to that, you will probably not have that thing yet. But, if you have deep issues that result from your upbringing, trauma, and abuse, you will not touch those things by changing the more surface parts, which are really just results or outcomes.

The process you are now in is one that is helping you to become whole a little more each day as you become aware and work on the structural integrity of your life and heart. This will automatically affect the world and others around you as you resonate with them, and them with you.

In the final two chapters of this section, we're going to look at persistent problems and how you deal with them.

18

DON'T STOP UNTIL YOU REACH THE BOTTOM
Get to the Heart of the Problem

When will this ever end?

It seems to be going on forever.

You've been digging for a while now, slowly stripping back the layers and allowing yourself to face up to whatever is revealed.

But there must be something wrong because it's taking longer than you expected.

You've identified main areas that seem to have the biggest effect on your life and you're committed to working them through.

What more can you give than you already are right now?

How do you keep going when you can't see an end to it?

Your Journey to the Core

If this is how you feel, I can relate. I've been there more times than I can count.

Most of us have lived on the surface of life for so long that we don't know any other way. When we engage with the deeper parts of life, we think we should be able to get results quickly with discipline and willpower. But there is a lot more to it than that.

We're taught to engineer life so that it works by all appearances. As long as nothing disturbs this, it can work well. But a consequence of this is that we have lost connection with some of the best bits of life as well, like the things that really excite us and bring us joy.

The motivation for this disconnection is usually buried deeply. And, even though we really know we're dissatisfied with the way life is, and crave change, that isn't enough to unearth the real problem.

If you dare to keep digging, the process will take you to the very depths of your being. This isn't just uncomfortable. It's hell. Literally! If you want to see the back of any problem, you're going to need to go to the very core of it – the point where the thing originated.

Imagine this with me: you've called a structural engineer to your house to look at that sinkhole you've discovered in your living room. They come in and say, "You've got a big problem." "Tell me something I didn't know," you think. "There's a giant hole between my sofas where the coffee table used to be." The engineer recommends patching it up with some mesh and plaster, then putting a rug over the top. It probably won't hold, but at least you won't have the hassle and cost of having to do all the digging up of the foundations to find the root of the problem.

That's ridiculous, right? It would never happen! But that's how we are with our *Structural Engineer* hat on. Because we're dealing with ourselves. And we treat ourselves differently to others. So, we simply cover over the chasm and push on.

Getting to the core means being willing to face whatever comes up and facing it until we have seen the back of it. At first, we don't have any capacity for this because we can only tolerate so much. Then, as we stay with it, our tolerance builds and we can face more and more.

I lived so much on the surface of life and focussed all my attention above-ground for so long, I had no concept of myself as a person whatsoever. As a result, I also didn't have any connection with my body. I didn't know until my 20s that my entire body was in a constant state of pain and exhaustion because I was so dissociated.

Getting in touch and learning to feel my body is a good example of choosing my own personal hell. I had been learning about grounding techniques and using connection with the body as the way to learn what I was feeling. As soon as I turned my thoughts to my body, it was like I had touched a live wire – the pain was so extreme. Gradually, over time, I could see that if I wanted a different experience of life, where I could enjoy living in the moment, I would have to get used to experiencing that pain.

As I became acquainted with the pain, I learnt to score it out of 10 as a way of connecting with my experience in the moment – 10 being the worst I'd ever experienced. From 2015 to 2020, I lived constantly between a 7 and a 9. Most nights were a 9, which helped me gain more understanding about why I struggled to get to sleep no matter how tired I was.

In November 2019, the crisis team and then the recovery team both employed the same scale for measuring my state because of trauma, anxiety, flashbacks, etc. Every day was a 10 or a 9 for months as I faced a constant barrage of anguish, having no idea how to keep going. Then, one day, in a meeting with my care coordinator from the recovery team, he asked me what my score was, and I said, "7." He highlighted what I'd just said and asked me how I felt about it. I wouldn't have noticed on my own.

It was one of the first ever moments of being able to see measured progress. I could feel the difference between the *10* where I had to fight suicide every second, the *9* where I felt like I had to get instant relief from alcohol, nicotine, diazepam and felt like I could just explode at any moment, and the *7* where I was feeling about the best I'd ever felt.

That last point is really important. I always thought that I'd need to reach bliss (or a score of 1) to feel like my life was getting somewhere and I could begin to enjoy it. But, for me, a *7* felt amazing, especially after month after month measuring *9* or *10*. I was sleeping better than I had in 30 years; I was in less pain; I was more present. Things made more sense to me. And the list goes on.

What I'm trying to convey with this example is that no matter where you are in life, a change of 'one' on any scale may just be the best thing you've ever experienced. If I compare the way I feel now to other people, I can quickly get despondent. I still don't get to enjoy life like other people. But compared to myself at any point in the last 40 years, I'm in heaven.

And that's what I mean by living your dream life. It's not some fantasy that you need to manifest. It is a deep and often simple desire you need to work your way towards. To be clear, I want to reach financial freedom. I want to have a large detached house on the outskirts of Bath with a plot of private land. I want to achieve business success. I want to be in a stable place when I bring children into the world. These are all in the 10-year plan and these are the kinds of things that money *will* buy. But, I am already living my *wildest-dream* life right now.

In fact, the life that I am living right now, compared to where I was 10 years ago, makes the dreams of achieving my financial and business goals seem like child's play. Nothing can compare to working through and beating addiction, to wake up in the morning without considering where my next drink or fix is going to come from. Nothing can compare to surviving a mental health crisis and being able to feel safe walking down the street on my own. And, nothing can compare to realising one day that I've had a week's worth of good nightly sleep for the first time in 30 years. Or belly laughing with my fiancée for the very first time. Or feeling completely present in a moment more often than before.

I've lost 84 lbs (38 kg) of fat over the last few years. My blood pressure has gone from 189/103 to around or below 120/80, my resting heart rate has dropped by 40 bpm, I have learnt to manage my personal finances so that I no longer haemorrhage money. The list goes on.

On your journey to the core, you may lose your way and become disillusioned, but just remember, there is no feeling like reaching the end of something that has plagued your life, and being able to live in the freedom that it gives you.

171

Change by Degrees

This process happens by degrees, like the sun gradually rising in the sky, warming you a little more the higher it rises. Then there comes that moment you realise you're no longer cold. But it doesn't happen in that moment, it's just that the temperature changes so gradually, you aren't aware of it taking place until there is discernible, measurable change.

The main reason the process must happen by degrees is because we cannot cope with too much at one time. Parts of us that can imagine the finished superstructure can often grow impatient because it seems so unnecessary that it's taking so long. But it is actually a kindness because facing and dealing with any more at one time would be overwhelming and potentially destructive.

One thing that I have seen in myself and others is how it can seem like you face the same things repeatedly. Each time this happens, it feels like a step backwards. The first time I realised this was when I was sharing with my brother-in-law how I felt completely stuck and wasn't getting anywhere. He said he understood why I felt like that, then told me all the ways I'd changed in the last year. This immediately brought perspective.

What I was experiencing was what some people call 'peeling the layers of an onion'. Each layer looks and feels the same. Each layer causes pain and makes it hard to see. But you really are getting down to the core, even if it doesn't feel like it.

Another example that's more fitting for our purposes is peeling back layers of mouldy wallpaper to discover rotting wood and crumbling plaster – as you go through this process, it may feel like you get weaker and weaker, and identify more and more problems. But each time you face up to and move beyond something, you will never have to face that exact thing again. You will face elements and aspects that feel and look the same, but it won't be the same thing. Then, like the moment you realise you're no longer cold, you reach a point where you are aware the problem is no more and you won't have to deal with it again.

One of the most important reasons we must go through this long process is because it is what gives us our autonomy. We have to choose every aspect of our lives. No one and nothing else can do it for us. The hard thing is that this was not the case when we were younger and, as a result, we unknowingly allowed things inside that are now standing in our way. We have to unlearn and un-choose those things in order to live free.

The good news is that by the time we're finished with a part of the process, we're able to stand on our own two feet and face whatever comes up in that area.

Change by degrees can be highly frustrating, but in the end, it will work for you if you allow it.

Unearthing Your 'Weaknesses'

In all your digging, you must dig until you find the point of origin of a problem.

If the origin is above ground, you need to look no further. But if the true source of your struggles is something that happened in the past because of your upbringing or trauma, you must get down to that level to see resolution.

On one of the deepest levels lies your worldview and how you see other people. As these things surface, you will notice patterns and connections in how you see the world and relate to others around you.

At the very core, you will find your own sense of identity – a sense that is largely formed because of the overt messages that you received growing up, the implied messages because of what you missed out on, and the abuse that compromises your view of yourself, making you feel like less than human and of little or no value.

Recovering these parts of us is the hardest and potentially the most dangerous work we can do. This kind of work has the potential to destabilise the entire building and cause everything to come crashing down. Which is why, again, I will recommend not doing this alone. And preferably get professional help.

You may wish you could go back to before the trauma ever happened or just wipe it from your past. This is completely natural. But, with the right perspective, you can actually come to peace about the beneficial effects that the trauma can leave you with after you've gone through the recovery process. I don't say this lightly, and I know this concept might seem heinous. Bear with me.

I titled this section using the word 'Weaknesses' in inverted commas because there is a twist to how the story plays out.

Once you have done the deep work, reached the very core, repaired the cracks, and seen the back of some issues, those weaknesses can actually become your superpower. Much like the broken bone that knits itself back together as you heal. Your 'weaknesses' can become the areas that you are stronger in than other areas. And, whereas before you were weaker than others around you, with nothing to give, you now have something to offer people that those who haven't experienced trauma can't fathom because of the process you've been through.

In Japanese culture, Kintsugi is the art of repairing broken pottery by mending the cracks with lacquer with silver, gold or platinum mixed in, highlighting the imperfections as part of the object's history.

This is a beautiful picture of what becomes possible in the life that has begun to heal. As the process completes in a particular area, we can come to where we no longer feel the need to hide from the things we feared and have brought us shame. We can deliberately draw attention to them because we are accepting or even proud that it is part of who we are. Secondarily to that is the knowledge that doing so can help other people.

Just a few months ago, I struggled to talk to my closest friends about being abused when I was younger. Now, I am sharing it with the world in this book. To be honest, I can't explain how this is possible other than to say that I have reached enough of a place of healing that it feels safe. And, more than that, I feel compelled to share it for my personal development and to help others.

Abuse and neglect, which led to Complex-PTSD, self-harm, addiction to alcohol and drugs, chronic pain and fatigue, and many other illnesses, were the banes of my existence for many years. The good thing about them is that they pushed me way outside all comfort zones to the start of this new life. Working through them has given me something to share. Who knows where I'd be without all that? Perhaps just living life on the surface with no knowledge of who I really am…

Post-traumatic growth is the technical term for what I'm describing. Once you've taken the time to work through the trauma and all its effects, you will see how the terrible things that were done to you have helped you grow and strengthened you.

After all that digging, you really will stand taller than you've ever imagined.

Toxic Positivity

I mentioned earlier the story about being corrected by someone when I was saying how unwell I felt. I call what they were doing toxic positivity because it is actually poisonous for everyone involved. It is one of the primary tactics to prevent the reality of our condition from being exposed and comes from fear. I'm not calling all positivity toxic. Just when it comes from a forced or coercive place rather than a place of liberty.

The simple reason people are trying to get others to 'be more positive' is because the expression of genuine feelings scares them. While they mean to help, it is actually a very cruel thing to do to someone that is baring their heart. After years of subjection to toxic positivity, I gave up and vowed never to trust anyone with the reality of what was going on inside me. Just yesterday, Clare asked me what was wrong, and I could only give my usual answer, "I don't know." She has to ask several times before I'm able to look at it and find the courage to tell her. I'm just waiting in fear for the correction that rehashes my honest expression with a 'positive' spin.

This is not something Clare often actually does. My expectation comes from emotional flashbacks. However, I often do exactly that to Clare. I give the classic guy response and jump straight to offering solutions, showing no understanding. When Clare expresses what she really wants from me, I can see my issue. When she expresses how she's feeling, it makes *me* feel hopeless because I had the idea drilled into me when I was younger that negative words will produce negative outcomes. So, I'm trying to rescue the situation as fast as I can. Even though it's coming from a good intention, it is still toxic and misses what is really going on with Clare. This is something I have to work on continually.

One therapist taught me about verbal ventilation – letting the pressure out of you by expressing everything you're feeling, which is wrongly seen as something that only women do. The two other best methods of releasing emotional energy from inside are crying and angering. Look at the way a baby expresses itself. One minute happily playing, next minute screaming blue murder, next minute laughing and dancing. Yes, but we're adults. We should know better. Yeah, maybe, but we don't! We are still undeveloped children inside in a lot of ways. The sooner we accept that and work with where we're at, the better.

I recently learnt that my grandfather on my mum's side was in the first wave of troops on the beaches on D-Day during World War II. There is a telegram from him he sent the first day from Sword Beach to my granny that ends with, "…still all tickety boo and nae bother at 'a!" Meaning, 'still all OK and no bother at all'. We all know today that all was not tickety boo. But he was trying to reassure his wife back home not to worry. Admirable.

But, like nearly all those who were fortunate enough to return, it seems unlikely that he ever got much beyond that assessment of how it was on those beaches. He became withdrawn and was frequently tearful, then succumbed to a series of strokes and heart attacks, dying young.

I am not saying that my grandfather did anything wrong here. And I'm also not implying that his letter from the beaches was toxic positivity. But what I'm pointing to is the British stiff upper lip that doesn't complain and just gets on with it. That *can* be toxic because of the effect it has on people that are desperate for someone to tell what they are really feeling. Like my grandfather. More and more, there is help for people that return from war, and an understanding that they are very unlikely to come out unscathed. They will need to talk about what happened and all its effects. This is not negativity, it is reality.

Ditch the toxic positivity and instead find people to be real with about what you're feeling. Then, you can start from where you really are and work your way to a more balanced life. It will be a weight off your shoulders.

Redefining Failure

Failure is one of the best parts of this process. It actually is one of the best parts of any process. It teaches you what doesn't work and shows you what you need to change.

However, for most people, failure is something to be afraid of. Usually because of the expectation of something bad happening as a result of perfectionistic tendencies. One way to see failure in a different light is to stop trying to get everything perfect and see it instead as an experiment. An experiment is a deliberate attempt to get things 'wrong'. You want to 'fail' because you know it is the only way you will learn anything and prove which way works best.

Think of a child from a loving family. When that child first pulls herself up on a chair, wobbles for a bit, puts her foot forward and then plonks down on her behind, her parents don't shame and ridicule her for falling over. They don't discipline her for her 'sin' or berate her for not trying harder. They delight in her because they are proud parents who marvel at how clever she is. She is experimenting with life and learning, and the bit that matters is that she took the step. The fall after is not what the parents will tell people about. Just the step.

As children, we are free to play and experiment to our heart's content, blissfully unaware of the pressures of life. However, as adults, there are consequences, and not every type of failure is the same. There are decisions we can make at forks in the road that will come back and bite us – the kind that we may deal with for a very long time. I have made too many of these decisions to count, and for a long time, I made myself feel better by putting it down to learning. But, by taking the time to assess a decision before making it, we can still learn but can also save ourselves a lot of unnecessary pain.

You can learn a lot by losing millions in a bad business deal and it makes a good story when you recover. But, you can also learn a lot by doing due diligence and *saving* yourself millions. Not such a sensational story. But the long-term effects will be profound.

You can learn a lot by getting into an abusive relationship and surviving to tell the tale. But, you can also learn a lot by listening to that alarm bell inside, saying, 'Don't do it!'

In mastering life, you can learn a lot by trying every trending hack and shortcut or by finding a new guru who claims to give you everything your heart desires in a one-hour session. But you can also learn a lot by taking life slowly and carefully in order to be kind to yourself, and give yourself the care you missed out on and deserve.

Redefine failure by building it into your life as a deliberate experiment. It can actually become something you look forward to because you know it teaches you so much.

Pulling the Plug is NOT Failure

Remember my example from earlier where I pulled out of helping to organise and perform at a charity concert? That was really hard to do. But it taught me that withdrawing from a commitment that I shouldn't have committed to in the first place – or can no longer commit to – is not failure. It is wisdom.

Same goes for my example of letting go of the flat in Bath. On the surface, it was giving up on a dream and added six months to the timeline. In reality, it was one of the best decisions I ever made – it probably saved my life, Clare's health, mine and Clare's relationship and a whole lot of financial pain. Since there's no way to prove a negative, we can't say what would have definitely happened, but I think it's clear that moving to a place where we couldn't pay the rent during the onset of a crisis would not have had a good outcome.

Pulling the plug on your commitments may cause disruption for both you and other people, but it can open up new possibilities that you couldn't see while you were still committed.

Unburdening as You Go

We often use the term 'baggage' to refer to our struggles. For example, "He's carrying a lot of baggage from his last marriage." As you go deeper towards the core, you will come across more and more baggage you've accumulated throughout your life. With your new essentialist mindset, you can start unburdening yourself from this added weight, which serves no purpose in your life plan.

My favourite picture for this is a runner who is training to win marathons. He trains every morning, six days a week. Rests for one day. He eats impeccably, sleeps eight hours most nights. He studies in his downtime, learning from the champions about running style, footwear, gait, pacing, and anything else that will give him an edge.

But, no matter what he does, he can't make it to six miles before collapsing. His knees are screaming and he's coughing his lungs up. His top is saturated with sweat and he loses electrolytes rapidly, making him feel even weaker. So, he studies more about running to improve his technique.

What's wrong with this picture? Nothing, right? Well, there is, but it's not obvious because I've left something out. His whole life he's struggled with his weight, carrying an unhealthy amount of excess fat, and no matter what he does, he can't seem to shift it. He's tried vegan, paleo, fat-free, calorie-controlled diets, but nothing works. He has been told by a doctor he must accept it as part of his life, saying, "It's probably just genetic."

For the entire time he's been training, he's been carrying 70 pounds (30 kilos) of excess fat on his body. It doesn't serve a purpose, and in fact, is affecting his entire system. Most of it is around his organs and has altered their normal function. His endocrine system is out of whack. Blood pressure through the roof. He is actually very unfit and unwell.

How can this be when he is so committed to running and dietary excellence? Because, so far, he has not identified the source of his 'baggage' – hidden carbohydrate intolerance.

When he discovers this term online and researches it, he limits his carbs and only eats the non-refined kind, in the state we find them in nature. He quickly realises which carbs he can tolerate and which he can't, plus the best amounts for health.

The pounds start to fall off and he sets a personal best during a morning run. His knees feel stronger, and he doesn't get out of breath anymore.

He makes his first 20-mile run and can see himself being able to enter a marathon in a year's time.

Like this aspiring marathon runner, we carry baggage around with us our whole lives. It serves no purpose other than to weigh us down. The cause often eludes us until, one day, we have a paradigm shift and it affects every aspect of our lives.

Excess baggage in your inner being is like excess fat on your body. If you let it get burned up as you go, you'll find you continually feel lighter and more able to do the things you've found so hard for so long.

What is Wrong with Me?

We have all asked this question. It becomes a problem when that becomes our default position – believing that there is something fundamentally wrong with us.

This was a question I asked my whole life. I looked at myself and the mess that I was in and couldn't find anything that made sense of why I was so out of control. I knew there were things like the violence of my dad and him dying when I was young, but as I dealt with these things, it still didn't get to the core of the problem.

In *Cracked Up*, the Darrell Hammond documentary I mentioned earlier, he shares his life experiences as a survivor of domestic abuse. After years of struggle, he was in a psychiatric facility where he met the first professional who understood him – Dr. Kotbi, a resident psychiatric at the facility – who said to him, "You are this way because of something that happened to you."[40] This stood in contrast to the usual messages he'd heard, which made him feel that there was something very wrong with *him*. After years of misdiagnosis, someone finally understood him.

---

[40] *Cracked Up: The Darrell Hammond Story*. Directed by Michelle Esrick, Ripple Effect films, 2018. Netflix, https://www.netflix.com/title/81162153

Hammond would later say, "People were approaching me as if mental illness was an airborne virus, as if this had come from nowhere and a bunch of drugs would fix it."[41]

Here's my take on this:

Don't ask what's wrong with me.
Ask instead what happened to me.

That is the antidote to treating yourself as if everything is your fault. When you finally get to the core, you will see that it all makes sense. You developed personas, ways of coping, crutches, personality traits to protect you from ever suffering what you did before. A lot of this was involuntary, unconscious, and unavoidable.

Bessel van der Kolk in the same documentary says:

"If you cannot tell the truth, you need to lock that reality away.
It becomes a splinter in your mind, a splinter in your brain, a splinter in your soul that starts festering. When your reality is not allowed to be seen
and to be known, that is the trauma."[42]

"If you cannot tell the truth…" he says. Well, how many of us have actually been allowed to? How many have had to lock it away for fear of judgement and punishment? That is the reason we conclude that it is *our* fault. Because others around us have told us it is. Despite the reality that it absolutely was someone else's fault.

---

[41] Maeve McDermott. "The Tragic Real-Life Story of Darrell Hammond." NickiSwift.Com, 2020, www.nickiswift.com/214433/the-tragic-real-life-story-of-darrell-hammond.

[42] *Cracked Up: The Darrell Hammond Story*. Directed by Michelle Esrick, Ripple Effect films, 2018. Netflix, https://www.netflix.com/title/81162153

Growing up, if I didn't accept that something was my fault, I would get beaten by my dad – a man who would never accept that anything was his fault. Ironic, huh? So, I learnt to absorb the blame for everything.

I'm sharing this because I want you to know that no matter how messed up your life is, no matter how out of control you feel, there is nothing wrong with you. It may be a while until you can accept that and see it for yourself, but it is still true.

When you see something in your life that's out of balance, ask, "What happened to me?" The answers to that question will lead you to the core and the solutions you're seeking.

Your History Matters

In the UK, we commemorate the end of World War I every November the 11th at 11 am by remembering all those who gave their lives for their country in wartime. We remember for many reasons, but the main reason is because we must never let ourselves forget those parts of history and the effects that it had on all involved. It mattered then. And it still matters today.

Your personal history matters in the same way. As I've mentioned, the church in which I grew up did not believe in counselling, but also did not offer an alternative. When my dad died, I had no one to help me navigate what I felt, and the confusing effects of his death. Within a short time, other people forgot, and it became a thing of the past, but not for my family, who still carry it to this day. If you've lost someone close to you, then you know what I'm talking about.

After World War II, many Germans were reluctant to face up to the reality of what had taken place in their country's name and their own involvement in it. The nation later addressed this denial and created a word for it – *Vergangenheitsaufarbeitung* – which means "working through the past". Instead of looking away and continuing to put the blame elsewhere, they chose the uncomfortable position of accepting their wrongdoing.

Sadly, the likelihood of your abusers reaching this place of humility that Germany has shown, as a whole, is unlikely. They are more likely to continue to allow the blame to remain with you, the victim.

Every November the 11th, we hear the phrase, "We will remember them,"[43] throughout the UK and across all media. Taken from *For The Fallen*, a poem by Laurence Binyon, it is a commitment to never forget the realities of the past.

When it comes to your life history, only you can say:

"I will remember."

What Stories Were You Told?

Before people developed methods of writing, stories were the primary method of passing knowledge from one generation to the next. Even though we have highly developed methods of communication, stories are still as effective as ever.

Stories can convey deep understanding, for example, *The Tortoise and the Hare*[44] discussed earlier. But they can also do great harm.

My mum's mum was very unsure of people of colour, even into her later years. Throughout her life, she only really encountered white middle-class people. And she was told as a little girl, by an ignorant nanny, that if she didn't behave, a black man would come in the night and get her.

---

[43] "For the Fallen Poem by Laurence Binyon." The Great War. Accessed 26 Nov. 2021. www.greatwar.co.uk/poems/laurence-binyon-for-the-fallen.htm.

[44] Aesop, and George Fyler Townsend. *Aesop's Fables – Complete Collection (Illustrated)*. 1st ed. Los Angeles, CA: CreateSpace Independent Publishing Platform, 2016. Kindle.

As *I* was growing up, I heard tales about gypsies coming to town, stealing everything and trashing the place. So, to this day, the word gypsy has negative connotations, despite one of my best friends being from a family of gypsies and someone I admire.

The stories I'm talking about in relation to your life are not what you'd normally think of when you hear the word 'story', but they are the things said and done to you which have all the elements of a story. The character is you but is often a fictional and inaccurate characterisation. You have themes, plots, subplots and so on. Hidden messages deep within the story can have a profound effect. Often, the people telling the stories don't realise they are causing harm. However, this doesn't lessen the effect. These stories warp your sense of self, make you suspicious of yourself and, ultimately, turn you against yourself.

One story I mentioned earlier was that, growing up, people made me feel everything was my fault. Another was that I was just like my father – the hidden message behind that was that I was controlling. I still find it hard to separate these ideas from my view of myself because they are so deeply ingrained.

When we're growing up, our brains are plastic and malleable. We are like sponges, soaking up the good and the bad. If the stories change during these early years, it may be possible to lessen their effects. As we get older, the stories and their messages become more entrenched and are harder and harder to untangle and dislodge. But it's not impossible. It just takes a great deal of work.

The stories that have the most effect come from a combination of the things that happened to you and what you were told about yourself. This contributes to your worldview. A large part of this process is making sense of the stories and rewriting them if need be, putting any blame firmly where it belongs.

19

MAKE SURE YOU'RE STILL IN IT WHEN YOUR TIME COMES

Win by Staying the Course

It's getting boring now.

You knew it would take time, but this is ridiculous.

It just feels like you're going around and around in circles.

And you wonder, "Why did I think it was a good idea to disturb what I had?"

"Was it really that bad?"

Each time you face something, you hope that this will be the last time, and then you'll be OK from now on. All you want is to make life work and get some results, but nothing seems to have made any difference that feels really satisfying yet.

It's just so much frustration.

Friends and family, who were supportive for a while, are worrying about you, and ask questions about when you're going to take steps to change the way you're feeling and start doing something different.

You watch person after person achieving their goals, and you're still stuck in the mud.

Surely there must be a better way.

The Eventual Superstructure

As I'm sure you realise by now, I believe this way is the best way forward. Because it works. The hard bit to accept is that it doesn't work straight away. It works once the process completes. And, as far as I can tell, the process is the process and takes the time it takes. Yes, we are in control of our lives and make choices every day that determine its course. But, with this process of change, it just seems to take longer than is comfortable, proportional to how constructive or destructive your life has been up till that point.

"But, that's not fair!" I know. I have faced this many times. Why do other people get to have it so easy? My best answer: because they do. But, although it is not fair, it is the way it is. So, we either come to terms with it or not. I know how hard that is.

If the process is the process, and being honest with ourselves, we can acknowledge that there's a lot of work to do before we can build anything of value, then it makes sense to prepare ourselves for a long adventure and learn to be satisfied with an eventual superstructure.

Just Waiting for Yourself to Be Ready

It's so easy to be hard on yourself because you feel you are not moving quickly enough, but that piles on loads of pressure.

I have another mantra for this: I'm just waiting for myself to be ready. It's got me through many hard times because it's an approach based on kindness. It is saying to yourself, I recognise that this is taking time because I am not yet in a place to change, make any decisions, or completely face this yet.

So, the next time you get frustrated with yourself for dragging your heels or seeming to take too long, just say to yourself:

"I'm just waiting for myself to be ready."

And you will be soon.

The Law of Inertia

The Borg, an alien race featured in *Star Trek: The Next Generation,* are famed for the expression:

"Resistance is futile."[45]

Darth Vader in The Star Wars movie, *The Empire Strikes Back,* says to Luke during their epic fight scene:

"You are beaten. It is useless to resist."[46]

But in both these cases, it was *not* futile. The Borg were defeated and Luke survives the battle, while Darth Vader is killed.

I said earlier that resistance is actually your friend. But in this heart process, it feels like it's holding you back. Something draws you in one direction and something else rises up to fight against us going in that direction. Or, we desperately want to see the back of something like addiction but can't escape its pull.

For many years, I saw this as something I was *doing*, but along the way, I came to see it as something happening *in* me – the law of inertia at work.

In physics, the law of inertia, stated simply, says that:

An object at rest remains at rest and an object in motion will remain in motion, maintaining the same velocity and in the same direction, unless they are disturbed by a force.

This refers to a physical object like a ball on a flat surface. If at rest, it will stay in the same position unless disturbed. If moving, it will keep moving forever until forces like gravity and friction interfere with its movement.

[45] *Star Trek: First Contact.* Directed by Jonathan Frakes, theatrical version, Hollywood, California: Paramount Pictures. 1996.
[46] *Star Wars: Episode V* - The Empire Strikes Back. Directed by Irvin Kershner, theatrical version. San Francisco, California: Lucasfilm Ltd. 1980.

And this universal law applies to our lives as well. Our life in specific areas, or as a whole, will remain at rest or head in a particular direction unless something or someone acts upon that state. This is one reason making life changes is so hard. It requires significant force (willpower, determination, habits, healing) to change the default position.

My interpretation of the law of inertia in relation to our lives is:

Everything achieved by effort must be maintained by effort. And everything achieved at rest can be maintained at rest.

The resistance we encounter during this process can feel disheartening because once we decide we want to change, we've got a fight on our hands. There are big parts of us that can seem to oppose all change, and this can make the entire process feel impossible. But, with patience, the stuck parts move and the out-of-control parts slow in response to the outcome we desire.

If your life is completely stagnant and non-productive, it will take a concerted effort to change that. If it is out of balance and heading in the wrong direction, the same is true.

But neither are a permanent issue. They both have their unique challenges, but you can overcome them both. The likelihood is that your life is a combination of 'at rest' parts you need to get moving, and 'fast-moving parts' you need to slow and bring to rest. And everything in between.

Inertia works against you when you're trying to move your life towards where you want to be. And, here's the good part: it works for you when something tempts you to change back again. The more you bring areas like addiction and mental illness to rest, the harder it is for them to get out of control again. And the more you get momentum with your dreams and things you desire, the harder it is for them to become stagnant again.

So, inertia really is your friend and built-in safety mechanism against unwanted change.

90 Degrees in the Wrong Direction

Andrew Wommack tells a story in his book, *How to Find, Follow, Fulfill God's Will*, about meeting astronaut, James Irwin, on a TV show where he discussed the lunar landing in 1969.

He recounts what Irwin told him:

"NASA basically threw the capsule towards the moon and every ten minutes for four days, they had to adjust their direction in order to stay on course. Sometimes the capsule was 90 degrees off from the direction it needed to be traveling, so they had to fire up the rocket to get back on track. Other times, they were just a fraction of an inch off. The flight path to the moon wasn't a straight line; it was a jumble of zigzags. Jim said they had a 500-mile-long target area for their landing. When he got out of the lunar module and stepped onto the moon, he was within five feet of being outside the landing zone. They nearly missed a 500-mile landing strip! But they still made it."[47]

Do you ever feel like you're 90 degrees off course? Or 180? I know I do. The amazing thing is, it doesn't matter. Even if you are heading at a million miles an hour in the wrong direction, you can still course-correct and get yourself back on track.

As with the lunar mission example, the best way to do this is to make lots of micro-corrections and not wait for some disaster to tell you that you need to change. If you make it a habit of your life to course-correct continually, the progress you make will amaze you.

---

[47] Andrew Wommack. *How to Find, Follow, Fulfill God's Will: God's Will for Your Life*. 1st ed. (Littleton, NH: Harrison House Publishers, 2013.)

When I started this process at 18 years old, I was heading in the opposite direction to where I hoped my life would end up. If you could watch a video of my life between then and now, you'd be able to see how much of the time I was 90 or 180 degrees out from my intended path. But, through constant correction, I found my way to the start of my dream life.

You will eventually reach the destination that you consistently head towards. So, go for it. And course correct as much as you need to stay on track.

Become Someone Who Can

One of my favourite things to say to myself is, "I can become someone who *can*…" Right now, I may be overwhelmed by trauma, unable to sleep, fearful that I won't actually finish this book. But I can become someone who *can* overcome all those things. This focuses attention on the now and on continual progress, rather than events and milestones. For me, it takes the pressure off because I don't need to be *there* yet. I am becoming someone who *can*, now.

You know there is a lot you can't naturally do. There is also a lot you've been conditioned against. But if you're patient, you can learn to be content with becoming someone who *can*… (*insert desired outcome*).

Becoming someone *who can* is a deep below-ground process that happens on the level of our sense of identity. A current personal example: instead of being a failure who achieves nothing (my lifelong story), I am becoming someone who *can*… write and publish a book. Clare and I became people who *can*… live in Bath… cheaply (which isn't meant to be possible). We gave our attention and effort to becoming people who could live in Bath and we ended up in Bath. We didn't end up in Calcutta, Madrid, or Liverpool because it wasn't in us. It was only in us to move to Bath and so we moved to Bath once we were fully ready. I know it sounds simple when said like that. And that's because it really is.

191

If you want something and you become someone who *can* have that thing, what can stop you? I'd say, 'nothing in the end'.

Here are a few ideas of what you can become to help you through your process and get you to where you can achieve your goals (and then I'll stop using the words *can* and *become* so much, I promise):

- Become someone who *can* <u>think</u> about <u>your dreams</u>
- Become someone who *can* <u>dream</u> about <u>your dreams</u>
- Become someone who *can* <u>talk</u> about <u>your dreams</u>
- Become someone who *can* <u>read</u> about <u>your dreams</u>
- Become someone who *can* hang out with people who also do all these things
- Become someone who *can* <u>take calculated risks</u> to achieve <u>your dreams</u>

Two areas from my life where I have become someone who *can* despite my natural personality, are timekeeping and organisation. I am an INFP personality type (according to the Myers-Briggs Type Indicator). Naturally, I do not think about time or space other than conceptually. I don't think about things. I think about ideas. Add to that my permanently dissociated, high-alert state and you get someone very disorganised, messy, and late. That was me while I was growing up.

In my teenage years, I learned my mum didn't like mess and other people hated it when I was late, especially if I kept them waiting around for me to arrive. I set out to change those traits, and with many years of effort, I now like things tidy and organised, and I am rarely ever late. If I know I'm going to be late, I message or call someone at the earliest point to let them know, giving them time to adjust.

There is almost nothing we can't change about ourselves, whatever our default position.

Can you see how this will make a profound difference to the direction and focus of your life? I hope so.

You Won't Be Down in the Dirt Forever

As I've said, I used the years of addiction and the time I was too unwell to work to prepare for the day when I could start building above ground.

Throughout the process, I held onto the hope that once the foundation was finally strong enough, the building would just fly up. This book is my first successful project – successful in the sense that I've seen it through to completion and it is out there making money for me.

I'm not saying any of this to boast (although I am very proud of it), but to say that, for me, this is the first solid evidence in business and creativity that this process works. I've seen it with my search for a partner. And I've seen it with where I want to live. But this business milestone felt way harder for me because of the stories I was told when I was younger – that it's wrong to want to be successful. And it's wrong to want money.

Every piece of the puzzle is now falling into place effortlessly. Nearly all of it I've considered or tried before. And anything new that I'm facing is easy to decide on because of the dry runs and practice runs over the years. It's overwhelming because it feels like a dream.

And that's because it *is* a dream. My dream.

I told you about the decision I made early in the process to stick it out, even if it took five or 10 years. Little did I know that five and 10 years would come and go, and it would be 20 years before I saw the results I was craving. Unless you can see how long the process will take before you get going, the only thing that makes sense is to commit to seeing it through, no matter the time it takes.

You will not build your superstructure overnight. You may not build it for a few years yet. But that's OK. If you take your time and build it strong, you'll only have to build it once, and it will stand tall for the rest of your days and beyond.

Perseverance

Perseverance is one of the most important traits you can develop. If I could highlight one factor that has helped me get to where I am, it's that. I have wanted to give up a million times. But I just kept going a bit further. And a bit further.

The only hope you have of getting to your dream life is to not quit until you get there. That sounds obvious just saying it, but in the moments when the dark clouds have consumed you, it is a hard thing to keep hold of. Perseverance is ultimately what will get you there.

My first business idea was an invention that filtered grey (rain) water to flush toilets and supply basins in bathrooms and toilets. I was 12 years old. I still have the NDAs I got people to sign when I pitched it to them.[48]

Twenty-two years later, with no business success to my name, I went into a service station toilet and there was my invention. A sign proudly stated how the system worked using filtered rain water and how much water it saved a year. Even though someone else had taken it to market, it was a great moment because it validated my earliest idea.

During my 10 years of on-and-off business projects, I abandoned at least five projects because I knew they would not work, or I knew I couldn't see them through. Now that I'm writing this book, I don't really care about all those years that I couldn't make anything happen. I am caught up in the stress and excitement of actually finally achieving something that is going to change my life forever.

How can I be so sure? Well, I can't. I didn't say I was certain. But I have a clear enough understanding of what's required to write and market a book after my years of learning, and enough self-awareness to know that I won't abandon *this* project. I now have enough confidence to tell

---

[48] One of the people I pitched it to was a friend from school who ended up becoming one of the richest young people in Britain when he was just a teenager. (He's a bit further ahead of me!)

the world that I believe this is the thing that's going to carry me over the line. Not the finish line. That comes in a few decades' time. This is just the starting line in business and creativity. The line where what's inside effortlessly produces what's on the outside. All the years leading to this point have just been the warmup and now I'm raring to get going.

I've got to admit, as I wrote those last paragraphs, I had a wave of nervousness come over me. I know I will look like a fool if nothing comes of this. But I'd rather be all-in when everything does fall into place. Being totally transparent with you, I have made these predictions many times before, only to be disappointed. But, a la Jack Reacher, I'm hoping and expecting with everything in me for success, and I have a plan for if it doesn't work out, which is… try and try again. And again. And again.

I'm not predicting success because I think I'm an amazing writer, even though I believe writing is one of my greatest strengths and something I've worked very hard on. My confidence doesn't have much to do with me at all, actually. It's based on the fact I can see how everything is lining up in me, and for me, to write, publish, and market this book. And I can't see any hindrance apart from the usual general ones I face most days, such as doubts, fears, and fatigue. But none of them have got the better of me for even a minute, which feels amazing because I've never experienced that before.

In relation to business and writing, the foundation is in place. It's solid, and every bit of it comes from the depths of my soul. As I write, I am being as honest as I can be, and I genuinely want to help you. If at any point I've changed something because I was concerned about what you might think, I've gone back and changed it back again. I think this book will be Marmite[49].

Most accounts of success only tell the best bits. They lure us into a false sense of security in our own life. I want to convey how arduous this

---

[49] UK slang for something that people will either love or hate which became popular after Marmite – a yeast-based food spread company – advertised "You either love it or hate it," as their slogan.

process has been for me. Not because I want to put you off, but the opposite. I want you to say, "If he can do it, then I reckon I can." And if you do, then I hope it will not surprise you when things seem to fall apart and then take a long time, maybe years to see progress.

From the point I realised I had a problem with drugs and alcohol, it took me 20 years to beat addiction, which was twice as long as I'd been alive at the point I got serious about quitting, and almost three times longer than I had spent being addicted.

Clare and I discussed business and dreams in the first weeks of being together. The vision didn't change, but it took six years and a lot of hell to see results.

In the end, we haven't come that far, if you just measure it on appearances. That's because the foundation is just a hole in the ground with concrete poured in. Doesn't look like anything special but it is vital. That foundational work is essential if you want success.

If you stay with this process, and stay with it again and again, you will eventually reach your destination. Expect that it will take you years or decades – and it won't disappoint you if it does. If it doesn't and you get to where you want to be sooner, it won't disappoint you either. You win either way.

Facing *Everything* That Comes Up

I believe that you already have everything you need to make it through and come out the other side of this process because I found what I needed in myself and have seen others do the same. Survival is hard-wired into our brains and hearts. The proof of that is you're still here despite everything you've already gone through.

The goals you wrote down in *Your 1/5/10 Plan* are enough to carry you through this entire process – they are the hope that one day you will get to where your heart longs to be. Somehow, in my own life, that hope was enough to get me through the seemingly endless years of struggle and pain.

As I've said, these ideas are not something I've concocted. Throughout history, there have been many depictions of this 'facing up to everything in you' that I'm talking about here – *Dante's Inferno, Dark Night of the Soul, Garden of Gethsemane* – they are all about facing your inner demons and overcoming the hardest inner trials.

Of all the hard things to do in this process, I know of nothing harder than facing the past and facing yourself. But stay with it and you will be greatly rewarded.

Delayed Gratification

This is another vital trait to learn. Along with perseverance, this sets you up for whatever may come your way. When life seems to go nowhere or crumbles around you, you can say that you will put off the thing you want until another day. Not for the sake of it. But because it serves you in the long term.

As you are digging and repairing your foundation, you need to take as much of the pressure off as possible. By allowing life to be what it is above-ground and not striving to change it, for the time being – except where it harms you or someone else – you give the best chance to the below-ground work.

Theodore Roosevelt said:

"Nothing in the world is worth having or worth doing unless it means effort, pain, difficulty... I have never in my life envied a human being who led an easy life. I have envied a great many people who led difficult lives and led them well."[50]

---

[50] Theodore Roosevelt. (1910) Theodore Roosevelt Papers: Series 5: Speeches and Executive Orders, -1918; Subseries 5A: Speeches and Executive Orders, -1918; 1910.

Another way of saying this is:

Everything worth having is worth waiting for.

It's true. Where I am now has been worth the wait. A few months ago, I was not so sure.

And like childbirth, once it's over, it's over and the pain dissipates. And the mother holds a beautiful baby that she's waited for patiently for nine months.

A famous experiment done in 1972 named *The Stanford Marshmallow Experiment* offered preschool-age children two choices of treat – a pretzel or a marshmallow. After the child had identified their preference, the adult observer explained the two choices the child had. Option 1: wait until the adult observer returned after leaving the room, in which case the child would get their preferred treat. Option 2: choose the least preferred treat at any point by signalling they wanted it to the adult.

Not surprisingly, the majority of children chose Option 2.[51]

Surprisingly, similar experiments performed on adults have yielded similar outcomes. It seems most of us haven't learnt how to wait for what we want even after we've grown up.

Learn to delay gratification and you will help your chances of success in the long term.

Sept. 7-1911, Mar. 29. [Manuscript/Mixed Material] Retrieved from the Library of Congress, https://www.loc.gov/item/mss382990694/.

[51] Angel Navidad. "Marshmallow Test Experiment." *Simply Psychology*, 2020, www.simplypsychology.org/marshmallow-test.html.

Maximising the Time You Have

If you have the perception that you are running out of time, I understand. I used to ignore people moaning about reaching 40 years of age because I thought they were being overly dramatic. But, as I approached my own 40th birthday a few months ago, I looked back over my life and found it unbearable to see how slow the progress had been. I had so little to point to. Then I remembered that 40 was the age that I had set years ago for many of my goals. Even though I now have a little over six months left before I'm 41, I have the confidence and drive to still achieve those goals in that time. If I don't though, I'll still be happy because I'm already happy with the life I'm living.

At 76, my mum is in a very similar place to me. We talk regularly and it feels great because we're now on the same wavelength and share a lot of the same realisations. I often think about how much harder it must be for her than for me to deal with the fact that her delaying of the process ate up so much of her life. The thing I try to encourage her with is that she's going to face this stuff regardless of whether she faces up to it, so she might as well face it. Maybe 'encourage' is the wrong choice of word, but I think it's good advice all the same.

One thing's for sure, you can't change your age. So, find whatever way you can to come to terms with the point you're at and, in time, you'll be too busy thinking about your amazing life to worry about your age.

Staying Stuck

During the process, there will be areas of your life that just seem to stay stuck, no matter what you do. Day after day, you'll hit up against them and there will be no discernible change. Why is this? Because those areas are encased in hardened concrete with tripwires and armed guards preventing anyone, even you, from getting near. The more stuck something is, the more it points to an area you need to treat with respect. It is more than likely hiding something that you are not ready to see yet.

I know how frustrating this is because I still have stuck parts that won't seem to budge at all. I just want to finish with that work so I can get on with life in that area. But, I'm learning more and more to be patient with the process and let it do its thing.

Do all that you can to make the most of life while the process takes place. My 2019 crisis revealed the final major obstacles from my past. I can now see that these realisations could not have happened sooner. If I could go back now and give *younger me* some advice, it would be, "The process is the process. You can't speed it up. You can only go along with it or go against it. So, choose the former as much as you can."

Be kind to yourself and learn to recognise when you are stuck for a very good reason.

Give yourself the time you need.

Structural Crises

Some cracks in our foundation are so deep and wide that no matter what we do to keep everything together, the building will still all come crashing down. I don't see this as a required part of the process, but a consequence of fighting against the process or not knowing how to go along with it. And unless our lives are secure with loads of support, we are highly susceptible to collapse. When even our will and desires are compromised and seem to work against us, a crisis is almost inevitable because we are so out of control. I lived in that place for many years through crisis after crisis.

Every crisis will be unimaginably hard, but it doesn't have to mean disaster. Like the difference between a bomb going off or a controlled demolition. One is purely destructive, resulting in carnage. The other has the end goal of construction and development. One has nothing in place to protect, the other is risk-assessed and mitigates against negative outcomes.

In 2004, I experienced a major crisis that was a total disaster. I reached such a desperate place that I just sat there and cried endlessly, saying over and over, as I often did in these times, "I want to die. I want to die." Internally, I had lost all hope and didn't feel I had anything to hold on to. It was the only occasion I needed to spend time in a psychiatric unit. The psychiatrist placed me on seven different lots of meds, including powerful antipsychotics. In my reviews with the psychiatrist, I tried to communicate what was going on inside me, but the psychiatrist didn't seem to understand.

Even though I survived it, my 2004 crisis was a disaster because I couldn't get myself out of the hole I was in and didn't have anyone who knew how to help me see what the core issues were. I was hearing hundreds of voices, most of which were harsh and vicious, keeping me in an endless cycle of having to act out whatever came to mind to get relief. I was so ashamed that I was so far gone and did everything I could to hide what I was experiencing.

When I came out of the psychiatric ward, I went abroad to do some aid work to give me something to focus on. Until that point, I had frequently cut myself with knives as a way of coping with the immense feelings of stress I experienced. While on a work break one day, a compulsion overwhelmed me to burn my hand with a lighter. I did it and it felt amazing. Because I could feel it. It got badly infected and made me ill, but I didn't care.

When I got back home, I came off all the medication cold turkey, as I always did, against the doctor's orders. I also stopped drinking. One night, I was in my bedroom and I had this moment of clarity that I had to punish myself. I pulled out my lighter and held it to my wrist. It hurt like hell, but I didn't pull away because I 'knew' I deserved it. In fact, I laughed because I knew I deserved it so much. That's what I believed anyway. Eventually, my wrist went numb and I finally stopped. I did the same thing one more time on the other arm and once on my stomach over the next few days.

Around that time, I had regular appointments with my GP to manage my mental health and medication. He asked to check the wounds and urgently referred me to a specialist. I went straight to the hospital, and the specialist said he would need to operate immediately. I didn't want that, and asked if someone could just clean up my wounds like nurses had previously done when I'd cut myself. The specialist said that I had burnt right down to the bone on both my arms and would die if I didn't have them cleaned out immediately.

What was wrong with me? Why was I so messed up? What kind of person does that to themselves? The kind that has been mentally and emotionally injured and still bears the scars that no one else can seem to see or help.

Almost exactly a year before my 2019 crisis, I had another one. Like the one a year later, it also seemed to come out of the blue. I was walking from my friend's house where I'd spent the evening. Clare had already driven back to her parents where we were staying. I had been drinking that night and went to a 24-hour service station to buy more cans for the walk back. My friend had given me directions on how to get home and I tried to follow them in my mind because I was too far gone to use my GPS and the battery was dying on my phone.

After a long time walking, I realised I was lost and had no idea what to do about it. This was not a new experience. It had probably happened hundreds of times in my life when I was drunk or high. But I wasn't just feeling the effects of being lost in the middle of nowhere in a physical sense. I felt it deep on the inside as well. I began whimpering and started saying, "I don't know what to do," repeatedly. It sounded familiar in my ears, but I wasn't with it enough to know why. I then started repeating, "Won't someone please help me?" But there wasn't anyone there to hear me.

After a while of walking in this state, I reached a bridge going over a motorway and felt this force pulling me towards the edge. I walked up and stepped over the small barrier that keeps pedestrians from getting too close to the edge. In the darkness, I cried like I'd never cried before, with the din of the cars passing by underneath. Wave after wave of agony crashing over me. I became more and more desperate, and at points, was petrified by the noises I heard coming out of my mouth. I've never heard anything like that before, or since. It was total desperation. Second by second, something deep inside fought the urge to just throw myself over. In my mind, a picture of me hitting the front of a lorry played on repeat. But a tiny part of me thought about my family, especially Clare, and what it would do to them. I eventually managed to call Clare to come and pick me up.

To this day, Clare says that what she heard as she answered the phone still haunts her today. I was like a lost child that had nobody and nothing to make him feel OK.

And that's exactly what I was at that moment. A year later, when new memories of being abused came back, I could see that all the emotions and sensations surging through my body on that bridge were because of that abuse. My heart's cries of, "I don't know what to do," and "Won't somebody please help me," were from that little boy.

I had an online session with my psychotherapist a few days later. I didn't tell her about the bridge because I was too ashamed and imagined she'd laugh and see it as silly. That makes me so sad now. How could I not know how much it mattered?

This crisis was a disaster because the only good thing to come out of it was that I made it off that bridge. I couldn't even see that as a good thing for a long time.

But despite their destruction when they happened, the bridge crisis, the 2004 crisis, and all the others didn't remain a disaster. I eventually made it to the core of the problem and there has been enough healing so that now my whole life is no longer completely dominated by the abuse that sparked all those crises.

I'm just realising that I didn't intend to share any stories in so much detail in this book. Partly because I don't want to trigger anyone or make them uncomfortable. As I'm wondering why I did share these accounts in that much detail, one answer for why is catharsis. That's my personal motivation. But I could do that elsewhere. The real reason I'm sharing it is because I want you to know that no matter how deep and dark the hole is you're in right now, you can get out. I can't prove that without also giving you my experiences to back the statement up. I hope this helps.

I've written the entire book up to this point feeling fairly level and detached, but as I've shared this last story, I've wept. That bridge still haunts me to this day because of the desperation and confusion I felt. It was terrifying. Apart from hope and love for my family, I still don't really know what kept me from that split-second decision to jump that would have finally brought an end to my torment.

No question, it was a disaster of a crisis. But look at where I've got to now despite it. Or is it because of it? That's the thing. Crisis, disaster, whatever. It can all be transformed and become part of the very fabric of your foundation. It can make you who you are. It can give you a connection with others. It can become the rock that your dreams are built on.

Sometimes, when things feel like they are falling apart, they are actually falling into place. Other times, they are just falling apart and if someone else doesn't step in, it may mean disaster. But if you can hold on a bit more, it will all fall into place.

How do you survive a crisis?

How do you survive a disaster?

Any way you can. That's it.

Find someone, anyone, to help you through it.

Take care of yourself. Don't mess with deep stuff. Surround yourself with good people that can help take care of you.

There is a way through it.

Never Settle Unless There's Something Worth Settling For

This is probably my favourite mantra.

Why do I keep dreaming? Why do I persevere?

Because unless there's something actually worth settling for, what's the point?
I want the same things many people do. I want to be married, with kids, in a house that I own, doing things I love, with the people that I love.

I'm not fully there yet. So, I keep going.

Getting to Bath is my favourite example of this, as you've probably guessed by now. When Clare and I got together, we decided we wanted to *be* together rather than have a long-distance relationship. On our journey to find somewhere to settle, we went from Bournemouth to London, to family, to Oxfordshire, to family again, before making it to Bath (after one stalled attempt).

The question is, "Was it worth it?" And the answer to that is a resounding yes. All those other places had their appeal or else we wouldn't have gone there. But the only place worth settling for was the one that was in us all along – Bath.

You have your own equivalent dreams. You may not know it. And it may be a while before you see it. But you have them.

You will reach resting places along the way that are not your dream destination, like the flat we're in at the moment. We have mostly settled here, but not completely. Most days, our detached house on the outskirts of Bath is at the back of my mind, reminding me that this isn't all there is. I'm happy to stay here for as long as it takes, but I am prepared to move at the drop of a hat if the opportunity arises.

Each time you hit a roadblock and wonder, "What's the point in pushing on? Why not just settle down and do away with all the struggle?" Remind yourself:

Never settle unless there's something worth settling for.

20

LOOK HOW FAR YOU'VE COME
Reaching Milestone Number One

It's finally happened.

The inner change that you've been dreaming about for as long as you can remember has finally happened.

You've persevered through endless battle after endless battle, and you've won.

You can clearly see that you're going to be free of addiction. Or, you realise you no longer feel bitter towards a family member who you've resented for years. Or whatever it might be.

You're a different person.

But then something bursts your bubble.

You share about the change with those close to you and realise they can't see it. They don't seem to know what you're talking about at all.

Did you make it all up? What if none of it's real?

Suddenly, you feel very confused.

Just A Bit Further

No question, this really is the first milestone and something to get excited about. But it is not your destination, no matter how much it feels like it. It is a foundational milestone. The goal is the building. So, you need to keep going a bit further.

The first few times this happened to me, I thought this was it. I had arrived. The change I'd been looking for was so real in my heart that I thought it would immediately produce the results I wanted on the outside. But weeks or months passed and nothing materialised.

The main reason for this is that there is opposition to the thing you are trying to build. That is anything that occupies the space where you want to place the building blocks of your dream life. Both things can't exist in that same space. And, because the former thing is already long-established, there is resistance to it being dislodged, and effort you must exert to achieve it.

The first glimpses of possibility are remarkable and you should celebrate them, but they are not the realisation of your dream. They will, however, give you everything you need to stay the course through to completion. Those glimpses are the hope that you can build all your dreams on.

Over time, I have learnt to have confidence in these milestones because it means the beginning of the end. It is the point where reality has overtaken perception and you are no longer under the spell that kept you captive.

But I have to tell you, it may get even harder from here. At least that's my experience. The reason I think it can get harder from this point is because the old and the new are smashing up against each other and the resistance to an altered state is immense. It can get so intense, it feels like everything is against you.

These are the *final fork in the road* moments when you have to choose what you're going to side with. What outcome you truly want. Choose with everything in you where you're going to spend the rest of your days – in a crumbling ruin or a towering superstructure.

I literally tried thousands of times to give up alcohol and smoking before succeeding. Sometimes my entire day was: buy some, try some, ditch it, repeat.

Then, one day, I could see myself as free. But it took years from that point, with a lot more inner work, for the picture on the outside to match that picture on the inside as everything in me finally lined up.

When I smoked my last cigar (yes, I rocked a Cuban) after having swapped them out for cigarettes, I got halfway through smoking it and just knew that this was it, so I flicked it on the ground. In that second, I got the event – the moment that everyone dreams about and the media showcases.

I have now reached the point where I'm concerned that, at my stag do, I may not want to have a cigar. Thinking about it now makes me feel a bit sick. I still have some of the same associations with it – something you do to celebrate with the lads on special occasions. But, more powerful is my desire for health and not needing substances to add to an occasion.

There are methods that claim to deal with these kinds of issues in weeks and even days. Do they work? I'm sure some of them do for some people. But when the underlying cause for those addictions or anything else is something much deeper, nothing but deep work will make a difference.

In 2019, immediately following the memories of abuse coming back, was the realisation that I no longer needed alcohol anymore because I had reached the core of that problem. However, that was just an internal milestone. It seemed completely real, but there was still stuff to work through and process before I could fully have it.

From that day, I drank more heavily than I had in many years as a reaction to the emotion and stress of the crisis. I quickly became physically dependent again and had to do a medical detox because it was too dangerous to stop cold turkey. From that point forward, I haven't touched another drop or even really thought about it. It's now been almost two years. It is no longer in me. I am no longer plagued by images and thoughts of alcohol and what it can do for me because the thing that caused me to need it has gone.

In the same way, after the memories came back, I knew I could finally lose the excess fat that I'd been carrying around for years. I think for me, it was just another way of insulating myself against the world. I am now the same weight I was when I was 20 – half my life ago.

I'll say it again: be prepared for the time that this process will take.

That concludes our section on digging down deep – the primary message of this book. At points, I have wondered if I should end the book here, but I think that would feel anticlimactic and unsatisfactory. So, I've included two more short sections to help with the fundamental above-ground work, which will lay out the framework that is eventually going to turn into your superstructure.

Onwards.

GET BUILDING

21

IN THE MEANTIME...
Getting by While You Wait

You feel you're getting closer all the time.

And you've passed many internal milestones

You still face obstacles, but they resolve more quickly and with less of a fight.

And you move on.

When you do *Your Structural Survey and Analysis* from time to time, you can see measured progress.

That feels great.

But, while you're digging down in the depths of your heart, life goes on.

So, how do you get by while you wait?

Your Inbuilt Survival Mechanism

Knowing how to get by while you wait for your dreams to materialise is actually easier than it may seem. You have an inbuilt survival mechanism that will sound a warning if you go too far wrong.

At the very least, you need to do what's necessary to stay alive. And, even though that's pretty obvious, it's still worth considering.
In survival, there is a rule of three. You can survive:

- About three minutes without oxygen
- About three hours in extreme conditions – heat, cold, etc.
- About three days without water
- About three weeks without food

Everyday life requires much more of us, especially when the aim is to thrive and get on well with other people.

In 2014, I had reached my lowest point physically and was sometimes only able to do one thing a day. So, there were days where I had to decide between washing or eating. When the smell got too much, that usually meant that I wasn't eating that day.

Many years before, at 12 years old, I was a millionaire in my heart. I had already got the image burned on the inside of me and could see it with everything in me. But I am not there yet. When it was only potential on the inside of me, it didn't automatically convert into being an asset to others – for example, to an employer who would then give me a cushy job with a fat salary.

So, along the way, when I could work, I had to wait tables, do hard labour jobs, cleaning, and many other things that are not in me to do – just to get by. That is what is required of you: whatever is necessary. Don't think that you are above anything just because you are choosing the deeper things of life.

We all need a place to call home, a safe-enough environment, food and water, adequate movement, work, money, connections to other people. When any of these are lacking, then our attention gets drawn automatically to trying to resolve them. You'll need to find your own balance and give the above-ground life whatever is required to survive while you're going through this below-ground process.

Sometimes We Need Crutches

If your leg is broken, you need a plaster and crutches. That leg suddenly becomes the most important body part and gets special attention day and night until it is whole again.

In the same way, when our heart or mind is broken, the broken part may need all our attention and we may need to use crutches.

I used all kinds of substances over the years to survive. And as wild as this sounds, they saved my life. Yes, they almost took my life on many occasions and have left a lasting effect, but they also protected me from having to face up to the unbearable, deadly pain of unresolved trauma before I was ready.

There is no easy way to handle giving up substances, or learning how to not self-harm, or anything that has inherent danger. The only advice I have is to trust yourself and if you must do it, do it as safely as you can. Or, if you can't trust yourself, find someone who you can trust to help keep you safe.

I'm leaning on coffee for the first time in months to get through the writing of this book. It grates against me because it makes me feel unwell physically and mentally, but something in me can't handle the long hours of writing without something to lean on. If I tried without it, it would take me months rather than weeks to complete this book because of how tired I get.

The word crutch is not a dirty word. If your heart or mind is injured or broken, you probably need crutches.

Don't be too hard on yourself.

How to Balance Life

Life can be so overwhelming that it can seem that the best we can hope for is fighting to keep our heads above water for the rest of our lives. This is an illusion.

In my blog post, *How To Balance Life: 7 Steps To Take Back Control*, I share a simple step-by-step plan to quickly get back on track when life seems overwhelming. I've included a lot of the advice from that post in this book and expanded on it, but the post puts it all together concisely.

The pictures most often used to represent balancing life are juggling balls or spinning plates. I like to see it as a sound engineer at a concert controlling the sound from his mixing desk. He is the most powerful person in the room even though most people won't know who he is. He can make or break the concert. And, he could kill the sound altogether.

Like the engineer controlling the sound at a concert, in your life, you are the most powerful person.

If you don't know how a mixing desk works, it just looks like a bunch of sliders and knobs that all appear the same. That's because they are. However, each knob or slider is assigned a job – one for treble, one for bass, one for a special effect, one for volume and a multitude of other factors.

Sounds pretty simple, right?

Wrong! If you think you can just learn the labels on the desk and get a job as an engineer, think again. It can take 10-15 years to master how to balance sound correctly.

Sounds a bit like another learning process, don't you think?

Another one of my mantras is "Just settings on a scale". I say this when I look at my life and feel despondent about where it is right now. Imagine looking at a slider on a mixing desk and feeling sad that it's at 0 or -100. You wouldn't because it just is what it is.

If we can see each aspect of our life as a setting on a scale, without judgement, and simply learn how to move that aspect toward the desired outcome, life will become more manageable.

If you want to hear more of my advice on balancing life, read my blog post, which goes into more detail:

https://www.digdeepstandtall.com/blog/how-to-balance-life-7-steps-to-take-back-control

But, one last point from the mixing desk picture:

Moving knobs and sliders is not what motivates someone to become a sound engineer. In the same way, balancing each aspect of life is not the desired outcome – it is only the means to achieve the outcome.

The master sound engineer elevates and embellishes the raw sound. Not by adding more effects and cranking the volume up but by being true to the sound, and sensitive to what will make it shine. Balanced with skill, it is symphony rather than cacophony and a feast for the ears.

In the same way, a masterfully balanced life is just enough of the right things to leave enough room to enjoy what truly matters, such as adventures, experiences, fun, family, friends and all the other things that bring joy.

The master sound engineer has learned through years of dedication and practice to become one with the mixing desk. And that is possible for you and your life. Think, 'Just settings on a scale', and learn to tweak and tweak and balance and balance some more, and eventually, you will come into harmony with your life and vice versa.

Start Small and Increase

As we've discussed in earlier sections, the only reliable way to learn anything is to start small and build on the results. The same is true with balancing life. An essentialist approach, from a place of knowing your 'why', will make this a lot easier because you'll have your guiding values in place and only be dealing with what really matters to you.

A life principle that is almost always true:

If you can't do the lesser, you can't do the greater.

That means that if you can't run five miles, you can't run 10. And if you can't go one hour without a cigarette, you can't go a day. Until something changes.

Get the most important area of your life working by tweaking it until it fits. Then add one more and tweak. Repeat.

Remember:

**A building a mile high
Begins with a single brick**

Hayward's Hierarchy of Tasks

Above, we looked at the basic human needs that are a requirement for survival. We must consistently meet these needs or we will struggle and eventually die.

If, like me, you have suffered with an illness or addiction, or anything else that makes life feel impossible, Hayward's Hierarchy of Tasks will help give you a framework for daily decision-making. But, before I carry on, I want you to replace my name with yours because Hayward's Hierarchy is just for me and yours is just for you.

I gave the example earlier about being so exhausted in 2014 that I had to choose between eating and washing. It was because of this that I came up with the tasks hierarchy.

For me, eating trumps washing. I'm sure the same is true for most people. This doesn't mean I don't like being clean. I do. Throughout my years of depression and addiction, I still showered most days, so deciding to not for a few days in a row was a hard thing for me to do.

I ate most days until the day I stank so badly or felt so gross that I had to shower. And this often meant not eating on that day.

On this level, it's quite easy to grasp. I only had enough energy for one task. The most important things most days were eating, drinking, going to the toilet, and cleaning myself. I did nothing else. On the very bottom level of my hierarchy pyramid, I had *drinking enough water* and *going to the toilet*. These felt hard, but were simple trips that I could leave to the last minute when I couldn't wait any longer. On the next level was *eating* and *showering*. For me, these felt much harder than fetching water or going to the toilet.

The tasks were not being chosen by how important they were to life, but how possible they were to me on any given day, which is subjective. I would go to the toilet and get water as infrequently as I could to conserve energy. And then decide each day, food or wash? Everything else was on higher levels and was not an option.

As my energy and capacity for tasks increased again, the next thing I faced was how to make decisions about seeing people. That was something that was decided *for* me when I was just in bed. But now I would have to decide between friends and my daily needs, which was a hard trade-off to make.

Partly because I'm a massive introvert and partly because of trauma, I have always found being around people requires the greatest energy from me. So, I learnt that when someone asked to see me, I would roughly think about what other things I had to do and gauge them on the hierarchy. Seeing a friend for a few hours could knock me out for days or a week, so I had to factor that in.

It's not a science – although I'm sure you could make it one – but the general idea is a priority structure that places certain things above others in terms of your time, energy, and values, and will help you make hard decisions as your life increases and builds to the point of being full of good things.

As you know, even the best things can still drain you and feel overwhelming. I have weeks when I look back and say, 'Wow, that was a pretty amazing week,' because I've done so many things that a few months beforehand I would never have been able to do. They are all things I want my life to be full of, like business, friends, exercise. But, they are still draining – and sometimes the most draining of all because I'm fully engaged with them.

As you go forward, trust in your inbuilt survival mechanism to keep you alive, learn to balance life by stripping everything back, starting small, and building up, and use [Your Name's] Hierarchy of Tasks to decide what you should focus on and eliminate each day.

22

THE PERSON YOU'VE BEEN WAITING FOR
Becoming Who You Really Are

What's that strange feeling?

Everything seems a little brighter than it did.

You keep noticing that you're handling life better. And people have commented on the changes they see in you.

When you look in the mirror, you see a friend. An ally. And someone you want to help.

You catch yourself just sitting sometimes. Not on your phone or watching TV. Just sitting. And mulling things over.

You feel more at ease with life and yourself.

The foundation is coming along and, although it's not finished, you can think more easily about exciting things to do with your life.

Instead of thinking about struggles and ideas all the time, you're thinking more about seeing friends and getting creative. Starting projects and joining clubs.

You're becoming yourself.

On the outside.

Laying the First Few Rows of Bricks

Congratulations! This is another major milestone.

Just as with a physical building, you don't have to wait until you've laid your inner foundation completely before you can build above ground. Whether you can build, and the height to which you can build, is more dependent on each individual area, even though there is overlap. If you're still in the place where there is nothing in you to do anything, as I was for years, just do what you can and go easy on yourself. I know it's hard, but I promise it won't be forever. There's still deep work to do that you're not aware of yet.

Although there is a massive amount of effort involved in above-ground work, this doesn't mean that when the time comes, you will have to go through and learn an entirely new process, starting from scratch. The beauty is that when the process has brought you to where you are ready to build above ground, you will have everything you need to do it and it will be automatic. It will just spring up from the ground, and sometimes, overnight.

Remember, the whole point of this process is to build a life – the life of your dreams. No matter how many people try to sell you some pseudo-spiritual mumbo jumbo that the only thing that matters is what's inside, you know you want a life worth living – and that means building something good that lasts. Not for show. But for fulfilment and contribution.

This is the bit that you've been dreaming about all your life. Where you finally get to focus on that house, that car, that job, that partner. On creating art that moves people, businesses that give jobs, and helping people in need.

It's not that it's ever gone away, you've just been focussing elsewhere because that made sense then.

But now…

Create Your Niche

There are a lot of cheesy platitudes (just my opinion) out there which major on how special you are and that you're the best thing ever. There is also a lot at the other end of the spectrum that aims to convince you that you're not special at all. I don't want to echo either of these viewpoints but lean more towards the first viewpoint.

How you *are* special is in the way your unique characteristics, personality, life experiences, interests, skills, talents, language, humour, and a lot more, make you different from everyone in history. This special quality is also true for everyone out of the billions of other people that have walked this earth.

Your uniqueness is one of the most important above-ground strengths in your S.W.O.T. arsenal. There is no one else who can see it like you do and no one else who can say it like you do.

That means that whatever you put your hand to, seek to do it *your* way. Not completely. That almost never works. But, within the life you choose for yourself, make it uniquely you.

Simple example: millions of people have written personal development books. Most of them have included personal examples of their own life to help the reader. Some of those will have experienced abuse, addiction and mental health struggles. However, not one of them can write what I've written because only I have the unique combination of a million ingredients that make up my particular life.

To write this book, I have learnt from some of the best about format, voice, and writing techniques, but if I copied their writing style and examples exactly, it'd be a pretty lame result. Not to mention plagiarism. This book is what it is because it's uniquely me.

Your niche is the narrow space only you occupy where you can be most yourself. If it doesn't exist yet, then invent or create it.

Let your imagination run wild. And become everything you know you can be that is uniquely you.

Own Your Successes

I've spent years hiding away, ashamed of my life and fearful of other people and their judgements. If you resonate with this, it is a hard thing to unlearn.

But once you see actual results above ground and you're building a life for yourself, it is something to be extremely proud of.

Some people will still be naysayers, even long after you've achieved success. Some people will maintain that life is all hard work and just about getting on with it. Smile and bid them farewell.

I think it's fair to say that most of the world isn't actively partaking in this process, so it is not a small thing that you have put in the work to get to where you've got to. It doesn't make you superior to them, but it is something worth celebrating.

You can learn more and more to own your own process and learn to stand tall as you become the truest version of everything that's in you.

You deserve to own your successes.

23

THE PATIENT BUILDER
Tactics to Avoid False Starts

You're blown away.

You can't believe where your life is now.

Everywhere you look, there's good stuff springing up, and it doesn't crumble. It remains.

It's just the start, but it's still exciting.

But, once you've been at it a while, you realise some bits don't look quite right.

And what you've built doesn't match the blueprint.

You worry because it feels like failure.

You thought you were doing so well.

Dry Runs

Don't worry! You are doing well. False starts are a part of the process, but there are a couple of things you can do to limit their frequency and effect.

You can plan every detail and actually think you've got it perfect, but that won't prevent false starts.

Most of the same principles that apply below ground apply above as well. You've got to allow yourself to make mistakes and learn. But, the consequences of certain types of mistakes can be greater above ground – like millions lost in a bad business deal. There are ways to mitigate against catastrophic losses while still taking risks and trying new things.

What I call a dry run is essentially a thought exercise that lasts as long as you decide to determine the best course of action. It's helpful when there are many options that, on first appearance, could all lead to where you want to go.

Either on your own or with someone you trust, talk through what each course will look like. Allow yourself to visualise it and think about how it will feel. This is simple but effective against blindly building a life that you have to backtrack from weeks or even years down the line. It keeps you on track with *Your 1/5/10 Plan*.

The other way you can perform a dry run is to reverse engineer it. Start out with the desired outcome of the goal you are building towards, and then think about what makes sense when you work backwards from the outcome to where you are now. When you have fully reverse engineered all the courses of action, one of them should best match your desired outcome.

Practice Runs

You won't ever really know when you're ready. No one does. Sometimes, you just have to settle on your best intuition and just go for it. *Going for it* can't be half-hearted because most things require an all-out commitment to work. So, you can't afford to hold back and expect results.

But how can you do that if you don't feel sure it's the best way?

Do a practice run. Pick the thing that has the most likelihood to get you to where you're headed but has the least investment in time, money, and energy, and the lowest risk if it doesn't work out. This is just a practice, so don't stress too much.

I have imagined hundreds of inventions, so while in bed in 2014, I tried to get one to market. It was a guitar pick (plectrum) holder that could hold a pick at an angle to the guitar, making it easy for the player to switch between fingerstyle and using the pick within songs. This is something I did frequently while performing, hence the inspiration. Many guitarists said they needed it and would buy it. It only cost me a few hundred to make a prototype, promote it, and set up the campaign to raise the funds for it.

The campaign didn't succeed, and I decided that inventing was not the route for me, at least not yet anyway. I ditched the project and moved on.

I could afford the time because I was unwell in bed. And, I decided up front I was comfortable with the cost, so I lost very little. Some of my other inventions would have cost tens of thousands or more to develop and taken years. That would have been too much for me at the time and didn't match my goals or values.

There are several other projects that I pulled the plug on over the years, and it was easy because I had performed a dry run and then decided while carrying out my practice run that it was best to pull out.

Practice runs make it easier to avoid biases like sunk-cost bias, which means that we continue to pour money into a business that will never work simply because we've already put so much in.

I have had many other ventures and projects, all of which were deliberate practice runs, or I relegated them to practice runs at the point where I decided it was not the way to go.

My mantra sums up this approach: Never settle unless there's something worth settling for. I knew those ventures weren't *it*, so I didn't settle.

Isn't that a waste of time? Couldn't I have been successful already if I'd just stuck with it longer? Well, that depends on the definition of success being used. I'm sure that I could have made something work in terms of business earlier and made some money. But, that alone is not a success for me, whereas what I'm working on now is success. Life has come together in such a way that I feel grateful I didn't settle earlier to get to what I'm now building in *Dig Deep, Stand Tall*. And none of the practice runs have gone to waste. They all help to form the current plan.

If you missed out on stages of development when you were younger, you may need to take some time to play and explore the world before getting too serious. This is easier to do if you are performing a practice run because it won't feel too heavy, as you've decided upfront that you are pitching it at a comfortable level.

Practice runs can save time, money, energy, and heartache in the long run. They are a less pressured way to approach new ventures.

Don't Litter the Earth

This concept is definitely controversial. I have approached business and creativity this way for several years. It may not be of use to you, but I'm sharing just in case.

I will build nothing for the sake of it if I can see that it has potential knock-on effects for other people or the world. In comparison, it is now clear by the effects on the world and everyone in it that the plastic industry must take responsibility for polluting our oceans and water supplies. I believe we should all take this kind of responsibility for anything we put out into the world and consider ahead of time the effect it will have on the earth and everyone in it.

When I was a kid, I would walk down the street eating a Mars bar – my favourite chocolate at the time – and when I was finished, just throw the wrapper on the floor and think nothing of it. I had no concept that it had any effect on the environment, or other people. One day, an adult saw me throw a Coke can on the floor right by a bin and they lectured me, baffled by why I would throw it down when the bin was right there.

In my 20s, people would talk to me about sustainability and recycling and I would either switch off or get annoyed. I saw them as zealots, doing their duty to convert me. Nowadays, I never litter. I buy the products that are truly sustainable and affordable as much as I can, and continually look for ways to improve the effect I'm having on the world and other people.

Part of the reason I couldn't hear what people were saying about taking responsibility for the planet a few years ago is because of my own struggles. It's hard to think about what washing up liquid to buy to lessen your impact on the environment when you are addicted and suicidal. But, the main reason was ignorance. I had never had it explained to me in a way that I could understand.

I believe it is healthy to consider the effects that our lives will have on the earth and others once we are in a place of being able to do so. I am especially thinking of creativity and business here.

In our digital, connected, microwave society world, we can churn out endless stuff, both physical and digital. And, not just the few who are creative types, but every single person who has access to a computer or a phone.

This makes it possible for me to lie in my bed with just a laptop and write a book that I can sell, market, and build a business around. Amazing!

But, it is also what enables us to litter the earth with stuff – physical and virtual – that amounts to noise that the rest of the world has to sift through to get to the good stuff.

To be clear, I'm not saying that you have to be the best in the world to create something and put it out there. But I am saying that I believe there is a way and a time to put things out there which will be the most beneficial for everyone affected.

Imagine someone puts their first art class painting of a landscape up on Facebook. It is clearly a beginner's painting. The perspective is wrong. The palette is bland. And it is covered in smudges. If they post it just to say *look what I did today*, it's just for people to share and enjoy, and that's great.

If they set up a free e-commerce site and start trying to sell it to make quick money, stuffing the site with keywords and ads, then promoting it to their same circle of friends on Facebook, I don't view that in the same light. It may be a step on the journey and a part of the learning process. And I accept that. But I don't think it should be encouraged or taught as a way for everyone with a phone to make a bit of money.

One reason I feel like this is because I have spent the last 25 years online and it is full of rubbish. Dross that you have to sift through to get to the good stuff prevents you from finding the thing that could help you get organised, start a viable business, or save your life in a crisis. And, again, I'm talking about physical and digital here.

Another reason I feel strongly about this is because I've worked for companies that simply don't care about their employees, treating them as commodities.

I worked hard for a cleaning company for a month, only to find out on payday that they hadn't paid me. After days of trying to get paid, I learnt they didn't have the funds because they'd grown too quickly and mismanaged their money. In the end, they went bust, leaving a trail of destruction and failing to pay many people what they owed to them. This is essentially daylight robbery. They knew they could not pay us and yet they still let us work for them, stealing our time and energy.

That cleaning company did an appalling job for the customer, didn't train people properly, and then failed to pay its employees. In what way did it really contribute to the world? Wouldn't the world have been slightly better off if it had never existed?

I think so.

And I'm not talking about sharks here that are just out to screw people over. I'm talking about good people that overestimated their abilities and got into something they shouldn't. Or, got in too early, and then got out when it suited them best, leaving the minions to suffer the fallout.

Can you tell I'm passionate about this?[52]

Money is often the primary motivator of these failed ventures. The problem is they are chasing the money without providing real value. But making money is easy. Providing real value is hard. And since we all need money to live, who's going to blame anyone for having a go and seeing if it sticks?!

My problem with 'just having a go and seeing what sticks' is that it is a blinkered viewpoint that doesn't consider the lasting consequences. I know that this point is idealistic, but it's something I think we need to be aware of to be able to avoid it and move things in a better direction.

I'm not talking about being restrictive and I don't want to rain on your parade. All I'm suggesting is that if you have an idea that you want to pursue, take a minute to consider the effects on the earth and other people. If it is simply self-serving, it's unlikely to do well anyway because people pay money for something that they value, and that gives them what *they* want. When you look back in a few years' time, are you going to see those things you did for the sake of it – without consideration of the effects – as something to be proud of? Or something you will regret having put out into the world?

Build with everything in you and don't stop building. Just be careful to not litter the earth with stuff that no one really needs.

---

[52] I think my passion for not littering the earth originally stems from growing up around all the junk my dad hoarded. I have a hatred for it and the lasting effects it had on my life.

A Change of Rules

This book is about principles of change. And you know by now that those principles can take a long time to establish in your life. Some of these principles are so consistent that you will view them as though they are laws that never change. This can make what I'm about to say next very confusing.

There will come a time in the process where what has been working for a while and yielding results is no longer the best way. And sometimes it requires doing the exact opposite of what was working before to make progress. Doing something according to the former principle, which had been consistently effective at producing results, no longer works.

The best example I have of this from my life is that for many years from 2011, I favoured and established the principle of rest in my life. It is one of the key principles I credit for turning my life around. I considered every decision I faced in the light of the principle of rest. If there were two options hard to choose between, I would favour the option that brought the most rest. Fast forward to a few months ago and rest was suddenly not the primary principle anymore. And when I say suddenly, I mean, one minute it was, the next it wasn't anymore.

The change happened when I received an email about self-publishing a book.[53] This was something I had considered for years, but I was missing pieces of the puzzle that I found in that email and the resources it shared. As I saw clearly what I needed to do to create a business and finally get it off the ground, the switch from rest to work happened instantly and I got on with making it happen.

---

[53] The email I received about self-publishing a book came from Jon Morrow at https://smartblogger.com. He was recommending https://self-publishingschool.com and founder Chandler Bolt's book on self-publishing. This book is in your hands because of what I've learnt from these two men. I will be forever grateful to them. If you want to know how to make money blogging, check out Smart Blogger. If you want to know how to make money self-publishing, check out Self-Publishing School. They are both the best resources I know of in their respective areas.

Whereas during my rest period, I would actively resist anything that felt like striving and would favour rest as much as possible, now I am pushing myself because I've entered a phase that is about above-ground growth, which requires an almost opposite approach. That doesn't mean rest has gone out of the window. It is the foundation for my newfound ability to build above ground.

Another example is that, for most of the months Clare and I were living with her parents, we allowed ourselves to be looked after and forget about responsibilities so we could deal with everything we were facing. Then, suddenly, one day it was in us to move to Bath and we sprang into action to make it happen.

When the rules change, it can feel very confusing, but if you're prepared, you can just take it in your stride knowing that all the preparation you've done has equipped you for the next part of the process.

24

THE MOMENT YOU'VE BEEN WAITING FOR
The Fulfilment of Your Dream

Massive congratulations.

This is the moment you've been waiting for.

You've actually built something that you can look at with your own eyes. And touch with your own hands.

It's completely *you* and you're proud of it.

There's still a lot about your life that's not where you want it to be, but you're not so bothered by it anymore because you've already got some results that were just dreams for so long.

You couldn't be happier.

And you don't really feel anxious anymore about whether the rest will work out because now you've got your undeniable proof that it's possible. If you can make it happen in one area, you're pretty sure you can in another.

You've started to see your dreams come true.

So, what's next?

Settling for Good Enough

When the thing that started as a glimmer of hope and a distant dream finally becomes a reality *out there*, it is literally the best thing ever.

It would be natural to think that the process going forward is to keep doing more of the same. But not only is that probably not sustainable in the long term, it's not actually necessary because you have found things worth settling for.

When I say to never settle unless there's something worth settling for, I'm not talking about waiting until you reach the ultimate destination, or 'perfection'. I'm talking about reaching the first iteration of your dream – the first thing that is in the ballpark of where you ultimately want to be.

If your dream is one that you can't realistically achieve for 10 years, like the goals that you'll complete at the end of *Your 1/5/10 Plan*, you are going to have a pretty miserable 10 years if you refuse to settle for anything at all before getting to that point. My best example is my dream house. It is large, detached, with land, an orchard, in the country. Right now, I'm in a one-bedroom flat which doesn't tick any of those boxes. But, it is still my home. It is the first iteration of my home and somewhere I am happy to be until I am ready to buy my dream house.

Some say good is 'the enemy of the best', but that doesn't sit right with me. Right now, good enough is the best thing I've ever experienced, and it is my friend, not my enemy. Good can be a step along the way towards the best, and I like that idea more. When I first started out, I was repulsed by *good,* let alone anything more, and could only tolerate tiny incremental changes. So, the idea of *good* being the enemy of the best just made me feel rubbish because I couldn't even handle *good*.

Remember that hostel I described earlier where the fire alarms went off all night and black mould covered the walls? Well, compared to that, our basic one-bed flat that's all our own is a virtual palace. We no longer feel desperately compelled to find somewhere to live. We are in the city we love, in a place that's good enough, and a million miles away from where we were. And we're still heading for more and bigger things, but will take our time because we've learnt contentment and patience along the way.

So, my mantra updated:

Never settle unless there is something good enough to settle for.

The End of an Era

The realisation of your dreams is monumental because it signifies the end of an era.

Getting together with Clare was the end of a very long era for me and the first above-ground success. I had gone through so many years of pining after girls without being able to tell them, telling them and having them reject me, missed timings, and the overwhelming belief that no one could ever want me. But, my dream was so strong that I kept going.

When it came time to share with Clare what I was feeling, I dared to put myself through it all again and it was so worth it. It was also the end of an era.

But that didn't mean it was easy from that point on. The first era with Clare lasted two years. Two years of us sorting through our baggage and navigating two traumatised people trying to live alongside each other.

But then, after that two years, a new era ensued. And so it has continued.

As the process has unfolded, something else has happened. The dream has faded and died.

And that's a good thing.

The realisation of your dream will make your dream obsolete. It will suddenly appear weak compared to what you now have. My dreams (fantasies) about a perfect wife paled in insignificance once I was in a real, loving relationship. The same goes for my dreams about finally reaching a place of independence from my family. Getting to my own flat with Clare in Bath was like nothing else.

And, at times, you'll pinch yourself. Not because it's so amazing, even though you'll have those moments. But because it feels so normal. And that will feel lovely after all the hell you've gone through and survived.

This won't happen all at once, but it *will* happen.

What Was All That About Anyway?

When you get to the end of the process in a particular area, it's over. And then no matter how hard the pain, how long the nights, it's hard to imagine what it was all about because the sting has gone and you've lost your connection to, and identification with, what you once were. It will feel like it's never been any different and every second of pain and struggle will become more and more irrelevant as you rest in what you've achieved.

Hard to believe? I understand that.

But I've seen it in so many people who have faced the most horrendous years of torment.

The thing is, when that part is healed, it's healed. Now, I'm not saying that you can reach a place where you are perfect and don't struggle anymore. But I am saying it's possible to reach that place in certain areas of your life, especially the ones you give the most attention to.

A lot of healing has happened in the couple of years since my 2019 crisis. The crisis fades further and further into the background. And, when I bring it to mind, it has less meaning and doesn't cause flashbacks like it used to. It has lost its power.

When I wrote about the crisis on the bridge, I said it brought up feelings that tell me there is still healing to happen. It's OK that I'm not fully healed yet. And, it doesn't stop me from living my dream life now.

If you stick with your process until you see the end of an era and the start of your dream life, you will genuinely look back and think, 'what was all that about anyway?'

Crazy, I know.

LASTING CHANGE

25

ONWARDS AND UPWARDS
Now You Own the Process

You're living the dream.

Not the Hollywood kind or the kind the gurus tried to sell you.

The one that you've chosen for yourself.

Not that it's really a dream anymore.

It's your only reality.

You've become comfortable with change and comfortable being uncomfortable. You wouldn't choose it, but you know it's part of life and you're OK with that.

You've got enough going on above-ground to keep you occupied and you're gradually digging less and less. You still check in with yourself regularly using *Your Structural Survey*, *Your Structural Analysis*, and the other tools in your toolbox. You're doing well.

So, What's Next?

Well, as always, that is really up to you and your imagination.

You've still got *Your 1/5/10 Plan* that you'll keep working towards and you'll be tweaking and updating it as you go.

As long as you keep allowing the below-ground work to continue, your foundation will sustain you as long as you're alive.

When you have dreams now, you know that you have confidence that you can make them work. And you continue to push the limits of what you can imagine for your life.

There is no restriction on what you can achieve in every aspect of your life.

As long as you continue to learn and grow, you can't go too far wrong. You're equipped for everything you might face – past, present, or future.

You're turning your focus outwards now and giving from a place of abundance.

You draw more and more people to yourself that resonate with you and can help you build your life. And you do the same for them.

You own your life and get to enjoy what you've built.

26

FRUITS OF THE PERPETUAL CYCLE
Enjoying the Benefits of Continual Growth

You are continually changing. Continually growing.

Your life looks and feels solid.

You're no longer the screw-up in your or anyone else's eyes.

In fact, many of your critics have come to you for advice because they know that you're the one who can help them in their time of need.

They see that you've grown and that you hold on to what you've built.

You've achieved lasting change.

They want that too.

A Growing Perspective

That's the aim, after all. Not just change. The world is full of that. It's easy to change in a heartbeat. And then change back again in the next. You've learnt to only be satisfied with playing the long game and seeing the process through with perseverance, and you're reaping the rewards.

As you build higher and higher, you will find your capacity grows with it and you can deal with things in real-time. Life will become more about the present with every passing year.

The higher you build, the further away you get from where you started, and the harder it will become to relate to what was so deeply ingrained in you.

You will dis-identify from it and it will no longer resonate.

When I get around people who are talking about drugs, I can't fit in anymore. I know people who can still do it, but I just can't because it's no longer in me. I find it hard to comprehend how I ever did them, especially the hard stuff. They scare the hell out of me now. It just shows me how desperate I was to need them every day, just to stay alive and not have to face the pain in my heart.

You will reach a place so far beyond where you ever thought was possible, and even though it's not a competition, you will overtake some people that used to intimidate you when you compared your life to theirs.

Life is still going to happen. Which means hard stuff is still going to happen. Other people are still going to be out of control and you'll crash into some of them from time to time, but you will show them more compassion and more understanding than you ever thought possible.

Get used to continually growing because it's here to stay.

27

HOW'S IT LOOKING FROM UP THERE?
Stand Tall, You've Earned it

No one believed in you.

At least, that's how it always felt.

You definitely didn't believe in yourself.

With the lot life handed you and the things that have happened to you, it's amazing that you've got to where you are.

Some people marvel. Others are envious.

You've served your time down in the dirt and you didn't quit until you'd done the work.

You dug deep and now you've earned the right to stand tall.

You should be proud.

Be Proud, My Friend

"But doesn't the proverb say that 'pride goes before destruction, a haughty spirit before a fall'?"[54]

Yes, but the pride it's talking about is an arrogant superiority over another person.

What I'm talking about is you having dignity about yourself and a sense of self-respect.

---

[54] Prov. 16:18. NIV

You have the right to respect yourself for what you've achieved and stand tall with a strong sense of your value.

You should be proud, my friend.

Rest in Your New Identity

The superstructure rests in place. Solid on its deep foundations. Buildings not at rest, move. And moving buildings crack. Cracked buildings crumble and collapse. That is the reason for all the work up to this point.

And now, you'll get to rest in who you really are. Your new identity. Although it's not really new. Mostly, it has just been uncovered and revealed. It is who you were already and you've just learnt to be comfortable living in it and expressing it.

But there's no denying that you are not recognisable from the person you were.

Once you've reached a point in the process where you've got enough substance *in* you, it will work its way *out of* you. You'll overflow with the things you've received and developed, and it will automatically influence the world and people around you.

Your focus will shift from the internal world to the external, and your desire to give to others what you've received will increase. You just won't be able to help yourself.

The more comfortable you become with who you are, the more you'll grow. The more you grow, the more you'll want to give. And the more you give, the more people will resonate with you and be attracted to you. This will be the point where you build your following and start leaving a lasting impression on the world.

It will still feel uncomfortable, like writing this book has been for me, but you'll rest in the knowledge that it's in you and it's got to get out of you. In fact, if you try to hold it in, you might just explode.

I think you're going to love who you'll become.

28

SOMETHING TO REMEMBER YOU BY
Leaving a Lasting Legacy

Imagine this.

You've come to your final moments.

Your loved ones are gathered around your bed.

No one is talking because there is a sense of reverence for the moment, and everything that needs to be said has been said.

You slip into an in-between place and start to look back over your life.

In the space of a few seconds, you see it all.

From beginning to end.

How Does That Feel?

Now, unless I caught you at a bad time, you're not actually there yet.

But how does it feel to imagine it? We talked about this concept earlier. Will you feel regret or will you feel pride in that moment? You can't know that for sure from this point, but you can imagine it. What still needs to happen for you to feel you've made the best use of your life?

The next question is:

What will you leave behind?

If you've done the work and allowed the process to guide you through to the end, you're going to have left behind a lasting legacy that will out-survive you by years.

One approach I've heard talked about in the last few years about how much money to leave behind in your will is to leave either none or very little. You time the dissolution of your assets in a way that leaves nothing or very little to your inheritors.

The explanation I've heard for this is to not handicap those you leave behind by taking away their own sense of autonomy – encouraging them to learn to stand on their own two feet. So, their view is that rather than a large inheritance being a gift, it could actually be a curse.

I understand this view, but I have a very different view on money, resources, and all other assets.

My parents had nothing. My dad had nothing to leave when he died apart from life insurance. My mum did everything she could to support me and went massively into debt to do so (I will finally finish paying this off in just three months. Wahoo!). I am still waiting to experience what it's like to have enough money to do any of the things I want to do. I don't want my kids to experience that.

I'm not just talking about money here either. I don't see the point in each of us working to build a life every day for 60+ years and then allowing it to dissipate and lose all that momentum and power. I see it as my duty and obligation to care for my family once I get to that point. My dream is to leave them with the understanding, knowledge, skills, and wisdom to continue from where I left off – not by doing what I think they should do with their lives – but giving them a platform to build what *they* want to build on. And this concept highly motivated all the work I've done over the last 20 years. I want to give my kids the best life possible. As much as it is down to me, I don't want them to experience what I experienced.

One of my favourite dreams is to leave a legacy so that many people can continue to benefit from what I've contributed long after I'm gone. The alternative is – dead, buried, forgotten. Or, 'we'd rather not talk about him'.

When you dissolve your assets, you split them apart and the money then lines who knows whose pockets to do who knows what with. If your children or any loved one who you want to pass your wealth onto have shown themselves to be trustworthy, you can guide them in your wishes for the money and leave behind a legacy that way. You can continue to do good long after you're dead.

It takes most people a lifetime to make a million. There's a lot of good you can do with a million pounds. Dissolve it and split it thousands of times among thousands of people and it dissipates and loses its power. All those years spent learning how to make and keep wealth undone.

As I've said, I understand the theory behind not wanting to hamstring the ones you leave behind by making them more dependent but, after you've read about my life, do you think I would be a good father if I wished the same thing upon my children just so they could learn what I've learnt? No way. I think the assumption in the viewpoint is that the kids will either squander it, or that they won't need it to get ahead. Neither is a certainty.

If my dad had left something behind, my mum wouldn't have had to work day and night to feed four children and end up in hospital multiple times from the stress. We could have gone on holiday. We could have bought clothes and had the things we liked. And we would not have lived in so much fear of money. I'm not blaming my dad, I'm just saying that's what motivates me to want to reach a different place.

There's obviously a balance to this, and everyone's choice will be different. For me, I hope I can give my kids some of the understanding from this book so they can build on what I've built so far and surpass me because of what I'm able to give them. I hope they can make more than I can make and give more than I can give, if that's what they want.

Why should each new generation start again like I had to? If you dig deep enough, and build tall enough, you'll have something to pass on to your children, grandchildren, or loved and trusted ones of your choice in future generations.

One of the main reasons I'm drawn to writing books and music is because of concepts like ownership, rights, and royalties. But, probably the main reason is that they are a way of giving value to the world and will outlast me. I love that. They are my lasting contribution. My legacy.

Once we're gone forever, we live on through the stories people tell about us. We can either be that scallywag who never gave an inch to anyone, or we can be the kind soul who would do anything for anyone. The miser who kept his fist tightly closed or the kind benefactor who left behind charities to help those less fortunate, or benches to sit before a beautiful view, or timeless music to continue to reach people with messages of hope. Or a fond memory of life and love.

This book is my lasting legacy to help as many people as I can. I want to go on record to say that it won't be my last and I expect to be writing another book soon to share about the people it's helped and how it's changed my life in terms of reach, income, and quality of life. I'm not being big-headed. Just being honest. That's what I want. And that's what I see. So, I'm saying it like it is. Like I've said, my confidence is in the process, not in myself. I hope that's clear by now.

Now, if the idea of legacy feels like 'pie in the sky', or you disagree with my view, I completely understand. No worries at all! If it doesn't resonate, smile and move on. You choose what's right for you. But, when you're ready, it is definitely worth getting clear on what you want to leave behind when you go.

Final Words

I hope this book has inspired you to choose a life where you dig deep so that you can eventually stand tall.

I am very aware that we've covered the whole process of life change in just a few pages. And I know you haven't gone through the process that quickly. In fact, you may still be deciding what you think about it all. That's fine. I am grateful you've stayed with me. I'm sure it has been difficult and I appreciate you taking the time.

As I write these closing words, it's been two years since my 2019 crisis. Clare and I are visiting her parents and I'm in the bed where I had those memories of abuse come back to me.

Today, we are going to view a potential wedding venue on the same day I'm finishing writing my first book. Life is good.

This process works.

I hope you choose it.

I believe in you and I'm cheering you on from the sidelines.

Go for it.

THANK YOU FOR BUYING MY BOOK!

If you enjoyed the book, I'd appreciate it if you would leave a review on Amazon and/or Goodreads!

Thank you

~Adrian Hayward

Acknowledgements

I am forever grateful to the following people.

Clare: for staying with me through the seemingly endless struggle, and holding on long enough to see it wasn't endless, after all. This book is your success too.

Mum: for demonstrating how to dig deep and face adversity, and showing me how to never settle.

My bro, Al: for dreaming with me about life's limitless possibilities. And the many hours you put into tidying up this book's first draft, giving me the confidence to complete it.

George: for consistently being a friend who's there for me, for being a sounding board for my ideas, and showing the same enthusiasm and encouragement for this book as the first creative ideas I shared with you more than a decade ago.

Bob: for being the friend who challenges my ideas, bringing fresh perspectives, and never failing to dig deeper. Our conversations always leave me feeling more inspired and hopeful.

Laura: for your painstaking and impeccable work editing and proofreading this book. Thank you for making me sound so much better than I would alone.

The BGS team: for helping to launch the book. Masa: for a cover design that I'm truly proud of. It captures the heart of the book beautifully and makes it pop. Marija: for your help in guiding me every step of the way.

And, finally, to the thousands of dreamers and thinkers who have shown me the way to look beneath the surface and find where the real treasures are hidden. I stand on your shoulders.

Author Bio

Adrian Hayward is the author of Dig Deep, Stand Tall – a message of solidarity and a guide to self-transformation for those yearning for a rich, fulfilled life. He believes in the wealth that's inside of us: our vital selves, our inner directions, and the intuition that guides us. Having overcome everything from abuse to addiction, homelessness, mental illness, and physical pain, he is passionate about sharing his learnings with anyone facing their dark moments. Adrian writes in a style that's hopeful, challenging, honest, and inspirational – and his one goal: to help as many people as he can to experience the profoundness of living a life of their dreams.

Connect with Adrian: https://www.digdeepstandtall.com/contact

Printed in Great Britain
by Amazon

77429829R00149